David Reid

G. Revie.
November 1940.

THE ASCENT OF F 6

by the same authors
The Dog Beneath the Skin

by **W. H. Auden** *and*
Christopher Isherwood

a tragedy in two acts

THE ASCENT
OF F 6

Faber & Faber Limited
24 Russell Square
London

First published in September Mcmxxxvi
By Faber and Faber Limited
24 Russell Square London W.C. 1
Second Edition March Mcmxxxvii
Reprinted September Mcmxxxvii
Fourth Impression January Mcmxxxix
Printed in Great Britain by
R. MacLehose and Company Limited
The University Press Glasgow

To
JOHN BICKNELL AUDEN

Ghosts whom Honour never paid,
In the foolish battle made,
Wandering through the stricken grove
Pluck the bitter herb of Love.

CHARACTERS

This play was first produced on February 26, 1937, at the Mercury Theatre, by Ashley Dukes *in association with the Group Theatre. Producer:* Rupert Doone. *Stage Designer:* Robert Medley. *Music by* Benjamin Britten.

Michael Ransom: William Devlin

Sir James Ransom: Raf de la Torre

Lady Isabel Welwyn: Ruth Taylor

General Dellaby-Couch: Erik Chitty

Lord Stagmantle: Edward Lexy

David Gunn: Barry Barnes

Ian Shawcross: Norman Claridge

Edward Lamp: Peter Ashmore

Dr Williams: Philip Thornley

Mrs Ransom: Dorothy Holmes-Gore

The Abbot: Evan John

Mr A.: Will Leighton

Mrs A.: Isobel Scaife

An Announcer: Stuart Latham

Wireless Singers:

Hedli Anderson

Alan Aldridge

Michael Lane

ACT I

ACT I

SCENE I

[*The Summit of the Pillar Rock, above Wastdale. Late afternoon.*]

[MICHAEL RANSOM *is seated, reading a pocket volume of Dante.*]

RANSOM [*reads*]. 'O brothers!' I said, 'who through a hundred thousand dangers have reached the West, deny not, to this brief vigil of your senses that remains, experience of the unpeopled world behind the Sun. Consider your origin: ye were not formed to live like brutes, but to follow virtue and knowledge.' [*Putting down the book.*] Virtue and knowledge! One can picture Ulysses' audience: a crook speaking to crooks. Seedy adventurers, of whose expensive education nothing remained but a few grammatical tags and certain gestures of the head; refugees from the consequences of vice or eccentric and conceited opinions; natural murderers whom a peaceful winter had reduced to palsied wrecks; the ugly and cowardly who foresaw in a virgin land an era of unlimited and effortless indulgence; teachers

13

without pupils, tormentors without victims, parasites without hosts, lunatic missionaries, orphans.

And glad they must have been to believe it, during the long uneventful voyage westward: yes, even
up to the very end, when the last deceptions were
choked from each in turn by the strangling Atlantic.
Who was Dante—to whom the Universe was peopled only by his aristocratic Italian acquaintances
and a few classical literary characters, the fruit of an
exile's reading—who was Dante, to speak of Virtue
and Knowledge? It was not Virtue those lips, which
involuntary privation had made so bitter, could
pray for; it was not Knowledge; it was Power. Power
to exact for every snub, every headache, every unfallen beauty, an absolute revenge; with a stroke of
the pen to make a neighbour's vineyard a lake of
fire and to create in his private desert the austere
music of the angels or the happy extravagance of a
fair. Friends whom the world honours shall lament
their eternal losses in the profoundest of crevasses,
while he on the green mountains converses gently
with his unapproachable love.

Virtue. Knowledge. We have heard these words
before; and we shall hear them again—during the
nursery luncheon, on the prize-giving afternoon, in
the quack advertisement, at the conference of generals or industrial captains: justifying every baseness and excusing every failure, comforting the
stilted schoolboy lives, charming the wax-like and
baroque, inflaming the obstinate and the odd and

14

all those hungry and cheerful persons whom the holiday now discharges into these lake-filled valleys radiating from the rocky hub on which I sit.

Beyond the Isle of Man, behind the towers of Peel Castle, the sun slides now towards the creasing sea; and it is into a Wastwater utterly in shadow that the screes now make their unhalting plunge. Along the lake shores lovers pace, each wrapped in a disturbing and estranging vision. In the white house among the pines coffee will be drunk, there will be talk of art at the week-end. Under I cannot tell how many of these green slate roofs, the stupid peasants are making their stupid children.

Nevertheless, let me receive such vigour as the impassive embraces of this sullen rock afford, from which no mastery can elicit a gratifying response, nor defeat sighs capable of despairing misinterpretation. Here is no knowledge, no communication, no possession; nothing that a bishop could justify, a stockbroker purchase or an elderly scientist devote years to explaining—only the voluntary homage paid by the living to the unqualified and dangerous dead. Let me pay it, then; pay it now, before I descend to the valley and all its varieties of desperation: the calculations of shopkeepers under the gasflares and the destructive idleness of the soldier; the governess in the dead of night giving the Universe nought for behaviour and the abandonment of the prophet to the merciless curiosity of a demon; the plotting of diseases to establish an epoch of inter-

15

national justice and the struggle of beauty to master
and transform the most recalcitrant features; the
web of guilt that prisons every upright person and
all those thousands of thoughtless jailers from whom
Life pants to be delivered—myself not least; all
swept and driven by the possessive incompetent
fury and the disbelief. O, happy the foetus that mis-
carries and the frozen idiot that cannot cry 'Mama'!
Happy those run over in the street today or drowned
at sea, or sure of death tomorrow from incurable
diseases! They cannot be made a party to the general
fiasco. For of that growth which in maturity had
seemed eternal it is now no tint of thought or feeling
that has tarnished, but the great ordered flower itself is withering; its life-blood dwindled to an unim-
portant trickle, stands under heaven now a fright
and ruin, only to crows and larvae a gracious re-
fuge. . . .

VOICE OF SHAWCROSS [*from below*]. Where are you,
M. F.?

VOICE OF GUNN. When you've finished saying your
prayers, we should like to go down!

VOICE OF SHAWCROSS. It'll be dark soon, if we don't
make a start.

RANSOM [*shouting back*]. All right! I'm coming!

    [*He begins to descend as the* CURTAIN *falls.*]

[*The* STAGE-BOX, *right,* *is illuminated.* MRS
A. *is discovered cooking.*]
MRS A. Evening. A slick and unctuous Time
Has sold us yet another shop-soiled day,
Patently rusty, not even in a gaudy box.
I have dusted the six small rooms:
The parlour, once the magnificent image of my
freedom,
And the bedroom, which once held for me
The mysterious languors of Egypt and the ter-
rifying Indias.
The delivery-vans have paid their brief imper-
sonal visits.
I have eaten a scrappy lunch from a plate on
my knee.
I have spoken with acquaintances in the
Stores;
Under our treble gossip heard the menacing
throb of our hearts
As I hear them now, as all of us hear them,
Standing at our stoves in these villas, expect-
ing our husbands:
The drums of an enormous and routed army,
Throbbing raggedly, fitfully, scatteredly, mad-
ly.

We are lost. We are lost.

[*Enter* MR A. *from work.*]

MR A. Has anything happened?

MRS A. What should happen?
The cat has died at Ivy Dene,
The Crowthers' pimply son has passed Matric,
St. Néots has put up light blue curtains,
Frankie is walking out with Winnie
And Georgie loves himself. What should hap-
pen?
Nothing that matters will ever happen.

MR A. No, nothing that matters will ever happen;
Nothing you'd want to put in a book;
Nothing to tell to impress your friends—
The old old story that never ends:
The eight o'clock train, the customary place,
Holding the paper in front of your face,
The public stairs, the glass swing-door,
The peg for your hat, the linoleum floor,
The office stool and the office jokes
And the fear in your ribs that slyly pokes:
Are they satisfied with you?
Nothing interesting to do,
Nothing interesting to say,
Nothing remarkable in any way;
Then the journey home again
In the hot suburban train
To the tawdry new estate,
Crumpled, grubby, dazed and late:
Home to supper and to bed.

18

Shall we be like this when we are dead?

MRS A. It's time for the news, John. Turn on the wireless.

MR A. I'm sick of the news. All you can hear
Is politics, politics everywhere:
Talk in Westminster, talk at Geneva, talk in
the lobbies and talk on the throne;
Talk about treaties, talk about honour, mad
dogs quarrelling over a bone.
What have they ever done, I ask you? What
are they ever likely to do
To make life easier, make life happier? What
have they done for me or for you?

MRS A. Smiling at all the photographers, smoking,
walking in top hats down by the lake,
Treating the people as if they were pigeons,
giving the crumbs and keeping the cake.
When will they notice us? When will they
flatter us? When will they help us? When
there's a war!
Then they will ask for our children and kill
them; sympathize deeply and ask for some
more.

MR A. Night after night we have listened to the ig-
noble news.

MRS A. We have heard
The glib justification of the sorry act.

MR A. The frantic washing of the grimy fact.

MRS A. But nothing to bring a smile to the face.

MR A. Nothing to make us proud of our race.

19

MRS A. Nothing we should have been glad to have
done
In a dream, or would wish for an only son.

MR A. Nothing to take us out of ourselves,
Out of the oppression of this city,
This abstract civic space imposed upon the
fields,
Destroying that tie with the nearest which in
Nature rules.

MRS A. Where we are unable to lose sight of the fruits
of our extraordinary industry.

MR A. And everything is emphatically provided:
The Dial Exchange and the voice of the lift.
We must accept them all and there is no one to
thank.

MRS A. Give us something to be thankful for.

MR A. Give it quickly.
I have read 'Too Late' in the hands of the office
clock.

MRS A. I have received singular warnings:
In the eyes of the beggar I have experienced
the earthquake and the simoom.

MR A. Sitting in the crowded restaurant, I have over-
heard the confabulations of weasels.

MRS A. Give us something to live for. We have waited
too long.

[*The* STAGE-BOX *is darkened.*]

ACT I

SCENE II

[SIR JAMES RANSOM'S *room at the Colonial Office.
On the wall at the back of the stage, hangs a large boldly-
printed map showing British Sudoland and Ostnian Sudoland, coloured respectively pink and blue. The frontier between the two colonies is formed by a chain of mountains:
one peak, prominently marked F 6, is ringed with a red
circle to emphasize its importance.*]

[*At a table covered with papers, maps and books
of reference are seated, from L. to R.* LORD
STAGMANTLE, SIR JAMES RANSOM, GEN-
ERAL DELLABY-COUCH *and* LADY ISABEL
WELWYN.]

[*As the curtain rises,* JAMES *lays down a docu-
ment from which he has been reading aloud to the
others.*]

JAMES. That, briefly, is the position. I think you'll all
agree with me that it is deplorable.

ISABEL. But surely, surely the report exaggerates? My
poor darling Sudoland—it's still like home to me,
you know! No, I simply can't believe it!

JAMES. We all appreciate your feelings, Lady Isabel.

They are most natural. Unfortunately I have reason
to believe that this report, so far from exaggerat-
ing, may even underestimate the gravity of the
situation. . . . From other sources—not official, it is
true, but as a rule absolutely reliable—we hear that
the whole southern province is in a state of uproar.
Government stores have been burnt, British officers
have been attacked. In a few hill stations, the
women of the European settlements have been
grossly insulted——

ISABEL. The cowardly fiends! How they can *dare*! In
my father's time——

GENERAL. In your father's time, Lady Isabel, a British
Governor was required to rule, not to coddle a
native population according to the sentimental
notions of a gang of home-bred politicians. The
Sudoese hillman has not changed since your
father's day: take him for what he is, he's a fine
fellow. He's a man and he expects to be ruled by
men. He understands strength and he respects it. He
despises weakness and he takes advantage of it. Show
him the business end of a machine-gun and he'll——

JAMES [*acidly*]. I think, General, you can hardly complain that the Government of which I am a member shows any lack of respect for your great practical experience in administration. Otherwise you
would not have been invited to attend this conference today. But I should like to suggest that, in
your wholesale condemnation of politicians, you are
apt to forget that we are only the servants of the

public. Public opinion has changed greatly, during the last twenty years, with regard to the native populations of the Empire. There have been unfortunate incidents which unscrupulous party agitators have not hesitated to misrepresent. . . . To take your own case, that most regrettable *contretemps* at Bolo-Bolo. . . .

ISABEL. Really, Sir James, is it necessary, at a time like this, to stoop to personalities?

JAMES [*smoothly*]. My dear Lady Isabel, I'm sure I had no intention of hurting the General's feelings. General, please accept my apologies. I only wished to remind you—not, alas, that any of us need reminding—how grossly a valued public servant can be maligned in the performance of a painful duty by the venom of the popular press—

STAGMANTLE [*beginning to laugh wheezily*]. *British General Butchers Unarmed Mob! Children Massacred In Mothers' Arms! Murder Stains The Jack!*

JAMES [*hastily*]. Yes, yes. . . . The nauseating clichés of gutter socialism——

STAGMANTLE. Socialism my foot! Why, that's out of the *Evening Moon!* Splashed it all over the front page—nearly doubled our sales, that week! No offence, General. We were out to smash the Labour Government, you know: and, by God, we did! Your little stunt came in handy: any stick's good enough to beat a dog with, you know! Ha, ha, ha!

ISABEL. Of all the utterly low and contemptible things I ever heard . . .

JAMES [*hastily intervening*]. As Lord Stagmantle quite rightly observes, the tactical problems raised by a great democratic electorate are exceedingly complex. One must try to see things in perspective. . . . I'm sure nobody doubts Lord Stagmantle's loyalty in this present crisis. Had it not been for his assistance in presenting the events of the last month to the public in their true proportions——

STAGMANTLE. Look here, Ransom; that's just what I came to tell you today. We can't keep this up for ever, you know. *The Thunderbolt* has been featuring the Sudoland revolts now for a week or more. How much longer do you expect us to play hush-hush? It's beginning to affect our circulation already. You've got to do something, quick.

ISABEL. But surely, Lord Stagmantle, all this suppression and misrepresentation of facts is a very mistaken policy? Why can't you have more courage? Why not let the public judge for itself? I should have thought that the truth——

STAGMANTLE. The truth, Lady Isabel, is that the natives of British Sudoland would like us to go to hell —pardon my language—and stay there. The truth is that we've got fifty millions invested in the country and we don't intend to budge—not if we have to shoot every nigger from one end of the land to the other. The truth is that we're under-garrisoned and under-policed and that we're in a blue funk that the Ostnians will come over the frontier and drive us into the sea. Already, they've spent thou-

24

sands on propaganda among our natives, promising
reforms which neither they nor we nor any other
colonial power could ever carry out. This revolt is
the result. . . . There's the truth for you: and you
want me to tell that to the public! What do you
take me for—a bolshevik?

JAMES. Lord Stagmantle is perfectly right: though,
with his characteristic flair for essentials, he over-
simplifies the situation, perhaps, a little. . . . He
asks me to do something. I shall not disappoint
him. I did not call this meeting merely in order to
alarm you. His Majesty's Government has a plan.
[*He rises and points dramatically to the map on the
wall, indicating F 6.*] The key to the problem lies
there!

ISABEL. Why, but that's the Haunted Mountain! I
used to be able to see it from my bedroom window
at the Residency, when the weather was clear. . . .
Let me think, now, what did the natives call it?

JAMES. The mountain has, I understand, many local
names; most of them unpronounceable. The survey
refers to it simply as F 6.

STAGMANTLE. A haunted mountain, eh? What's the
story in it?

JAMES. Merely that the mountain is said to be haunted
by a guardian demon. For this reason, no native
will set foot upon it. As you will notice, it stands
exactly on the frontier line. Both Ostnia and ourselves claim it; but, up to the present, no European
has ever visited the district at all.

25

ISABEL. I remember, when I was a little girl, being afraid that the demon would come and carry me away with him to the top! Aren't children absurd?

GENERAL. May I ask if we came here this morning to discuss fairy-tales?

JAMES. A fairy-tale, General, is significant according to the number of people who believe in it. This one is credited by several millions of natives on both sides of the frontier. . . . Also, the legend has lately developed a sequel which may appeal more strongly to your imagination: The natives have begun telling each other that the white man who first reaches the summit of F 6, will be lord over *both* the Sudolands, with his descendants, for a thousand years.

STAGMANTLE. Aha, so that's their little game! The Ostnians started this yarn, of course?

JAMES. You are very quick to follow me, Lord Stagmantle. And perfectly correct. Yes, the Ostnian agents have been propagating this story for the past six months. We've traced it right down into the plains.

GENERAL. But, Ransom, you don't seriously suggest that the Ostnians expect to gain anything by spreading this absurd nonsense? The hillmen may believe them, I admit—the Sudoese are credulous beggars—but, hang it all, what good can it do Ostnia? None whatever. If you ask me, this is just another Ostnian bluff. Bluffing's their strong suit.

JAMES. I wish I could agree with you, General. But this morning this telegram reached us, through the

26

Intelligence. [*Reads.*] Expedition under Blavek left Ostnia for Ostnian Sudoland yesterday great secrecy intending attempt ascent of F 6.

ISABEL. Monstrous!

GENERAL. The beggars are mad as coots!

STAGMANTLE. Not so mad as you may think, General. I ought to know something about propaganda stunts: this is one of the best I ever struck. If the Ostnians get to the top of F 6, your natives are going to make big trouble. Whether you like it or not, you'll have to start shooting. And Ostnia will intervene, in the name of the poor oppressed subject races. They'll have world opinion on their side, into the bargain. . . . You're in a cleft stick.

ISABEL. Can't we send a cruiser to stop this expedition?

STAGMANTLE. Certainly. If you care to start a European war.

GENERAL. At any rate, these chaps will never reach the summit.

JAMES. We can't be too sure of that, I'm afraid. There's a great deal at stake.

ISABEL. You sit here calmly and say so! Oh, if only I were a man! What are you going to *do*?

JAMES. His Majesty's Government proposes to send an expedition to Sudoland without delay.

ISABEL. Oh, good! Good!

STAGMANTLE. Now you're talking!

GENERAL. Never heard such damned tomfoolery in all my life!

27

STAGMANTLE. I must congratulate you, Ransom. You're on to a big thing—a big thing for all of us! The *Evening Moon* will subscribe two thousand to the funds of the expedition . . .

JAMES [*shaking hands with him*]. I knew we could rely on your public spirit, Lord Stagmantle!

STAGMANTLE. . . . provided, of course, that we get the exclusive rights—pictures, film, lecture-tours, story. We can discuss details later. . . .

JAMES [*rather taken aback*]. Er, yes, quite so, of course

———

ISABEL. And now, there's not a moment to be lost! We must think quickly: who are you going to send? How will you find the right man to lead them?

JAMES. I am happy to say that I have found him already.

ISABEL. You've found him! Oh, Sir James, I think you're wonderful! Who is he?

JAMES. My brother.

ISABEL. You have a brother! And we never even knew!

JAMES. My brother Michael is considered, by competent experts, to be one of the best climbers in this country.

ISABEL. How I should adore to meet him—the man who can save Sudoland!

JAMES. We'll go to him at once. My car is waiting. [*To* GENERAL *and* STAGMANTLE.] You'll come with us, I hope?

GENERAL. I refuse to be a party to this wild goose chase. When you have ceased to occupy yourselves with demons and need some serious advice, you will find me at my club. Good morning.

ISABEL. Oh, General!

[*The* GENERAL, *taking no notice, goes out.*]

STAGMANTLE. Never mind him, Lady Isabel. . . . A remarkable old gentleman, but conservative: no vision. He'll come round to the idea in time. . . . [*Rubbing his hands gleefully.*] Well, Ransom, let's see this brother of yours! I'll write the interview myself! By George, what a day for the *Evening Moon*!

ISABEL [*reprovingly*]. What a day for *England*, Lord Stagmantle!

STAGMANTLE. Oh, England—yes, quite so, of course. . . . [*Looking up at map.*] The Ascent of F 6!

[ALL *three of them stand regarding the map in reverent silence as the*——]

CURTAIN FALLS

29

[*The* STAGE-BOXES, *left and right, are illuminated. In the right* BOX, MR A. *sits listening to the
radio* ANNOUNCER, *who speaks from the* BOX *on
the left.*]

ANNOUNCER. If you drink coffee for breakfast, you will
be familiar with Sudoland as the name of one of the
most delicious brands in the world, said by con-
noisseurs to be equal even to Blue Mountain and
only half the price. But, unless you have a brother
or a nephew there, I don't expect you know much
more about this beautiful and exciting country. It
is about as big as Ireland and embraces a wide
variety of scenery and climate, from the moist hot
river-plains in the north to the magnificent escarp-
ment of mountains on the southern border. The
natives are delightful people, of wonderful phys-
ique and very humorous and artistic. Their villages
consist of mud huts and they live very simply,
chiefly on boiled bamboo shoots, which they call
KHA. Most of them are employed on the coffee
estates, where they make excellent workmen. You
may have read recently, in some of the papers, of
riots in Sudoland, but from personal experience I
can tell you that these stories have been grossly ex-
aggerated. They were confined to a very small sec-

tion of irresponsibles egged on by foreign agitators. Hospitals, clinics and schools have done much to raise the standard of personal hygiene and education among the Sudoese and the vast majority are happy and contented.

[*At this point*, MRS A. *enters the* STAGE-BOX, *right, bringing coffee.*]

If ever I make enough money to retire from journalism, it is to a small hill-station in Sudoland called Fort George that I should like to go, to spend the evening of my days. I have knocked about the world a good deal and seen most of the famous views, but never have I seen anything to compare with the one you get from the English Cemetery there. From this point you see the whole mountain range which culminates in that terrifying fang of rock and ice called so prosaically on our maps 'F 6', but in the native tongue 'Chormopuloda'—that is, the Haunted Mountain. There are many legends about this mountain and the troll who lives on the summit and devours all human beings who dare approach it. No Europeans have, so far, ventured into this region, which is barren to a degree and inhabited only by monks who resent foreigners. These monks practise a mysterious cult which is believed to be descended from the religion of Ancient Egypt; and there are wonderful tales current of their mystical and psychic powers. Be that as it may, I do not think it likely that it will be long before our young climbers will discover a new ground for their

31

sport, offering more magnificent opportunities for
their skill and their love of nature, than even those
afforded by the Alps or the Himalayas. . . .

[*Exit.*]

MRS A. It's all very well for him, he can travel.

MR A. Cousin Bertie's boy was there;
Poor lad, he had to come home last year:
They've reduced the staff on his coffee estate.
He said that the people and country were great.

MRS A. Why do you never take me abroad?

MR A. Darling, you know that we can't afford . . .

MRS A. Afford! It's always the same excuse—
Money, money!

MR A.   Dear, what's the use
Of talking like this?

MRS A.   You don't really care;
If you did, we shouldn't be here.
Why don't you do something, something that
          pays;
Not be a clerk to the end of your days?
A dreary little clerk on a dreary little screw—
Can't you find something proper to do?
But you don't care, it's the same to you
Whether I live or whether I die.
I wish I were dead!

MR A.   Mary, don't cry!
You never know, perhaps one day
Better luck will come our way:
It might be tomorrow. You wait and see.
But, whenever it happens, we'll go on the spree!

32

From the first-class gilt saloon of channel-
   steamer we shall peer,
While the cliffs of Dover vanish and the Calais
   flats appear,
Land there, take the fastest train, have dinner
   in the dining-car,
Through the evening rush to Paris, where the
   ladies' dresses are.
Nothing your most daring whisper prayed for
   in the night alone—
Evening frocks and shoes and jewels; you shall
   have them for your own.
Rome and Munich for the opera; Mürren for
   the winter sports;
See the relics of crusaders in the grey Dalma-
   tian ports;
Climb the pyramids in Egypt; walk in Ver-
   sailles' ordered parks;
Sail in gondolas at Venice; feed the pigeons at
   St Mark's....

MRS A. O, what's the use of your pretending?
   As if life had a chance of mending!
   There will be nothing to remember
   But the fortnight in August or early Septem-
      ber,
   The boarding-house food, the boarding-house
      faces,
   The rain-spoilt picnics in the windswept places,
   The camera lost and the suspicion,
   The failure in the putting-competition,

The silly performance on the pier—
And it's going to happen again next year!

MR A. Mary!

MRS A. Don't touch me! Go away! Do you hear?
[*She bursts into tears; he shrugs his shoulders
and goes out, slamming the door. The* BOX *is
darkened.*]

ACT I

SCENE III

[*Parlour of a public house in the Lake District. Shabby late Victorian furniture. A window at the back gives a view towards the fells. By the door, L. is a telephone. On the right, a cottage piano. After supper.*]

> [*At a large table, in the centre of the stage,* MICHAEL RANSOM *and the* DOCTOR *are playing chess. At a smaller table, L.* LAMP *is bending over a microscope. In an armchair, R.* SHAWCROSS *is writing in a notebook.* GUNN *is at the piano, strumming and singing. As he writes,* SHAWCROSS *frowns with suppressed annoyance.*]

GUNN [*singing*]. The chimney sweepers
> Wash their faces and forget to wash the neck;
> The lighthouse keepers
> > Let the lamps go out and leave the ships to wreck;
> The prosperous baker
> Leaves the rolls in hundreds in the oven to burn;
> The undertaker

35

Pins a small note on the coffin saying 'Wait till I
    return,
I've got a date with Love!'

And deep-sea divers
    Cut their boots off and come bubbling to the top,
And engine-drivers
    Bring expresses in the tunnel to a stop;
The village rector
    Dashes down the side-aisle half-way through a
        psalm;
The sanitary inspector
    Runs off with the cover of the cesspool on his
        arm—
To keep his date with Love!
        [*Jumps up from the piano and goes over to*
        SHAWCROSS.]
Still sweating at that old diary?
SHAWCROSS. I was doing my best to, in spite of your
    filthy row.
GUNN. So glad you enjoyed it, dearie. I'll play you
    something else. [*Goes back to piano.*]
RANSOM. Shut up, David. [*To* DOCTOR.] Check.
GUNN [*leaving piano and looking over* SHAWCROSS'
    shoulder]. Hullo, what's all this? [*Reads.*] '. . . fol-
    lowed up a splendid short pitch to the north sum-
    mit. Gunn, as usual . . .'
SHAWCROSS [*snatching book*]. Leave that alone, damn
    you!
GUNN [*grabs book back and reading*]. '. . . Gunn, as usual,
36

fooling about, completely irresponsible. I can never understand M. F.'s patience with him. . . .'

[SHAWCROSS *tries to snatch book.* GUNN *dodges round the chair.*]

SHAWCROSS. Give it here, blast your eyes!

GUNN. Ha, ha! Wouldn't you like it! Why can't you be patient with me, like M. F.?

SHAWCROSS. You little fool! Do you want me to hurt you?

RANSOM. Give it back, David. [*To* DOCTOR.] Check.

GUNN. Sorry, Ian. You're not cross with me, are you? Come and have a drink?

SHAWCROSS. Surely you ought to know by this time that I never drink the day before a climb.

GUNN. To hear you talk, one'd think we were a lot of monks.

SHAWCROSS. It just happens that I take climbing seriously. You don't.

GUNN. All right. Keep your hair on. No offence. [*Strolls over to* LAMP.] Let's have a squint, Teddy. [*Looks into microscope.*] What's this stuff that looks like mouldy cheese?

LAMP. If I were to tell you, you wouldn't be any the wiser.

GUNN. No, I expect I shouldn't. [*He wanders over to watch the chess players.*]

SHAWCROSS. M. F., may I take your climbing boots? I'd like to oil them for you.

RANSOM. It's very kind of you, Ian; but I gave them to the maid.

37

SHAWCROSS. I wish you wouldn't, M. F. How can you expect a girl to oil boots? I'll just do them over again, myself.

RANSOM [*smiling*]. You spoil me, Ian. One day, you'll regret it. I shall become as helpless as a baby without its nurse.

SHAWCROSS [*blushing*]. It's no trouble at all. I like to keep things decent.

GUNN [*yawning and stretching himself*]. Gosh, I'm bored! If I had a thousand pounds, I'd buy an aeroplane and try to fly across the Atlantic: if I had five hundred pounds, I'd go to Africa and shoot lions. As it is, I've got seven and elevenpence, so I suppose I'd better get drunk.

> [*As he moves towards the door, the telephone rings.*]

SHAWCROSS. I expect that'll be the man about the new ropes. [*Goes to telephone.*] Hullo. . . . No, it's a call from London. [*To* GUNN.] For you.

GUNN. Ask who it is. Wait a minute. . . . Don't, for Heaven's sake, say I'm here!

RANSOM [*To* DOCTOR]. Look out for that castle, Tom.

SHAWCROSS. Who's speaking? [*To* GUNN.] It's a lady. A Mrs da Silva.

GUNN. Gosh, that's torn it! Tell her I've gone away! Tell her I'm dead!

SHAWCROSS [*listening*]. She says she knows you're here and that it's no good saying you aren't. [*Holding out receiver to* GUNN.] Here, take it! I'm not going to do your dirty work for you.

38

GUNN [*after making frantic signals, advances gingerly to the telephone*]. Oh, hullo, darling—how lovely to hear your voice! No, of *course* not! How *could* you think so! Well, you know, I'm terribly busy just now. I *could* get up to town this week-end, if it's really absolutely necessary. . . . No, darling, I *swear* there isn't! Listen, here comes a kiss! *Good*-bye! [*Hanging up receiver and mopping his forehead.*]And now *she's* on the track again! Says her husband's going to divorce her! Oh, whatever shall I do?

SHAWCROSS. I hardly see what else you can expect, when you've got about as much self-control as a tom-cat. . . . What we do object to is the way you involve us all in your nasty little intrigues.

GUNN. Everybody seems to be finding out my address. This morning, I had five more bills. . . . Oh, if only I could get right out of England for six months, they might forget about me.

RANSOM. Check.

DOCTOR [*making a move*]. Aha, M. F., that's got you! . . . No, it hasn't. . . . Oh, dear!

RANSOM. Mate. Thank you, Tom.

DOCTOR. Why do I always do something silly when I play with you? It's no good. You get me every time. [*Rising.*] Oh, I'm so fat, I'm so fat!

GUNN. Doc., I believe you forgot your exercises this morning!

DOCTOR. As if I ever forgot them! As if I ever could forget them! [*Sighs.*] Perhaps it would be better if I stopped them altogether. But I haven't the nerve.

39

GUNN. Poor old Doc.! Come and have a drink. Whisky shrivels up your flesh.

DOCTOR. Do you really think so? I've got to a stage where I can believe almost anything.

[*A knock at the door.*]

ISABEL'S VOICE. May we come in?

GUNN. Another woman! Don't open it, for the Lord's sake! Let me hide! [*Dives under the larger table.*]

[SHAWCROSS *opens the door. Enter* LADY ISABEL, *followed by* STAGMANTLE *and* SIR JAMES RANSOM.]

ISABEL [*to* JAMES]. I told you they'd be in here!

RANSOM [*unpleasantly surprised*]. James!

JAMES. Ah, Michael, there you are! Very glad to find you at home. I thought I'd pay you a surprise visit. I've brought some friends who were anxious to meet you. . . . May I introduce my brother—Lady Isabel Welwyn, Lord Stagmantle.

RANSOM [*with a rather stiff bow*]. How do you do? These are my friends—Doctor Williams, Mr Shawcross, Mr Lamp. . . . David, come out. . . .

[GUNN *scrambles out from under the table.*]

Mr Gunn.

GUNN [*politely*]. How do you do?

JAMES [*to* RANSOM]. I've been telling Lady Isabel and Lord Stagmantle about your climbing exploits. They were greatly interested.

ISABEL. You know, Mr Ransom, you're not a bit like Sir James! I should never have taken you for brothers, at all!

40

STAGMANTLE. It's a great pleasure to meet you, Mr Ransom. I'm always glad to make contacts with prominent personalities, in any walk of life. Sir James tells me that you have many sidelines. You're a scholar, I believe? Well, now, that intrigues me. Scholar and man of action: an unusual mixture, eh?

JAMES. As I never fail to observe, my brother has all the brains of our family. In all humility I say it—my brother is a great man.

RANSOM [*who has listened to the above remarks with growing uneasiness, now turns on* JAMES *and blurts out*]. Why have you come here? What do you want?

JAMES [*smiling awkwardly*]. Hardly very friendly, are you, Michael? How do you know that I want anything—beyond the pleasure of seeing you again after so long?

RANSOM. How often, when we were boys, you used to come to me as you come today, with that peculiar smile on your face, half impudent, half timid! What do you want this time—my toy engine, my cricket bat, my rare West Indian stamps? Or shall I do you a favour—run that errand to the butcher's, correct your Latin verses, clean the motor-bicycle? Let's hear what it is, James: we're grown men now.

JAMES [*with a change of manner*]. You are quite right, Michael. I shall not waste words. There is no time to lose. [*Lowering his voice.*] Isn't it possible for me to speak to you alone?

41

RANSOM. If you have no secrets from your friends, I have none from mine.

JAMES. Very well, since you wish it. . . . [*Clearing his throat.*] In the name of His Majesty's Government, I have come to make you a most important proposition——

RANSOM. Which I unconditionally refuse.

JAMES [*taken aback*]. But—Michael—I haven't even told you what it is!

RANSOM. You have told me quite enough. I know your propositions, James: they are all alike. They are exceedingly convincing. They contain certain reservations. They are concerned with prestige, tactics, money and the privately pre-arranged meanings of familiar words. I will have nothing to do with any of them. Keep to your world. I will keep to mine.

JAMES. You are not being fair to me, Michael. You have never been fair to me. What I am offering you is an opportunity—the greatest of your whole life—to do something after your own heart. We want you to lead an expedition which will attempt the ascent of F 6.

RANSOM [*startled*]. F 6! What have you and your world to do with F 6?

JAMES. Ah, you see, Michael; I told you you would be interested!

RANSOM. Since boyhood, in dreams, I have seen the huge north face. On nights when I could not sleep I worked up those couloirs, crawled along the eastern

42

arête, planning every movement, foreseeing every hold. Through how many thousand years have those virgin buttresses been awaiting me! F 6 is my fate. . . . But not now. Not like this! No, no, no! I refuse!

JAMES. But, Michael, this is sheer caprice! I must explain: the future of England, of the Empire, may be at stake. Weighty political considerations, the Government——

RANSOM. And your own career? Be honest, James, and add the heaviest weight to the scales. . . . No, I am sorry, but F 6 is more important to me even than that. I will not go.

ISABEL. Mr Ransom, if you lead this expedition—no matter whether you succeed or fail: and of course you *will* succeed—there is not a woman in England who will not feel proud of you—*more* than proud! I appeal to you, as an Englishwoman, in the name of all Englishwomen. You refused your brother. Can you refuse *me*?

RANSOM. I can refuse you, Lady Isabel.

ISABEL. You disappoint me, Mr Ransom. Sir James made me hope great things of you. He was too generous. I had never expected this. I see it in your eyes. You are afraid.

RANSOM. I am afraid of a great many things, Lady Isabel. But of nothing which you in your worst nightmares could ever imagine; and of that word least of all.

STAGMANTLE. Look here, Ransom; let's understand

43

each other. I'm not going to talk a lot of blarney to you about England and Idealism. I'm a practical man. You're a practical man—of course you are! Only failures are idealists. My dear fellow, think what this climb will mean to you! Cash, and lots of it! You need cash to pursue your hobby? Of course you do! Look at it in a sensible light. [*Lowers his voice.*] Between ourselves, this expedition's nothing more or less than a political racket. You know that. So do I. Well, who cares! Leave the dirty work to your brother and me: we're used to it. Forget about us. Go out to F 6 and enjoy yourself. Make climbing history. By God, I envy you! If I were twenty years younger, I swear I'd ask you to take me along!

RANSOM. I like your reasons best, Lord Stagmantle. And I respect you. You talk like a man. I'd rather have you in front of me on a rope than behind me with a loud-speaker. . . . I am sorry. I know you won't understand my refusal. But I do refuse.

STAGMANTLE. Is that your last word?

RANSOM. It is.

[*There is a knock at the door.*]

STAGMANTLE. Too bad. . . . Well, Ransom, it seems we shall have to look elsewhere.

JAMES [*triumphantly*]. Not yet! [*He goes to the door, opens it and speaks to someone outside.*] Ah, splendid! So you got my telegram? Yes, he's here!

[*Enter* MRS RANSOM.]

Here is somebody who may be able to persuade you, Michael!

44

RANSOM [*with a cry of dismay*]. Mother!

MOTHER [*advancing to* RANSOM]. Michael, I am so
proud——

RANSOM [*recoiling*]. You too! No, it is impossible!
You come so late, it is an accident
Your shadow adds to theirs, a trick of the light.
If this was purposed——
> [*In the course of the following dialogue, the light
> becomes entirely concentrated upon* RANSOM *and
> his* MOTHER. *The rest of the stage is darkened:
> the other figures being seen only as indistinct
> shapes in the background.*]

MOTHER. I have no purpose but to see you happy,
And do you find that so remarkable?
What mother could deny it and be honest?
I know my son the greatest climber in the world;
I know F 6 the greatest mountain in the world.
May not a mother come at once to bring
Her only gift, her love? When the news came,
I was in bed, for lately
I've not been very well. But what's a headache
When I can stand beside my son and see him
In the hour of his triumph?

RANSOM. If I have triumphed
It is not as you think. I have refused it.

MOTHER.
Refused it? Why? But no—I must not question
My grown-up son. You have your reasons, and I
Shall try to trust them always.
James, I remember——

45

RANSOM.

> James! Was there no other name you could remem-
>> ber,
> No niece or cousin? Ever since we were born
> I have heard the note of preference in your voice:
> And must I hear it now? When we could barely
>> walk,
> I watched him romping through the children's
>> party;
> When we were boys at school,
> I saw him charm his way to every heart
> And idly win the prizes.
> That would not matter; we are older now
> And I have found myself. But James who has
> The gaping world to ogle with his speeches
> Must fill the last gap in his great collection
> And pot-hunt for his brother. Years ago
> He stole my share of you; and must he now
> Estrange me even from myself?

MOTHER.   Michael,

> There is a secret I have kept so long
> My tongue is rusty. What you have said
> I knew and I have always known. Why do you
>> start?
> You are my Michael and I know my own:
> A mother has no heaven but to look.
> That was your secret; there is also mine:
> From the good day when both of you were born,
> And I first held you both in my two arms,
> James, bigger, prettier, the doctor's pride,

46

Responding promptly to the nurse's cluck,
And you, the tiny, serious and reserved,
I knew your natures. You never knew your father:
But I can never see James toss his head
Or laugh, or take a lady's arm, but I
Must see your father in his popular pulpit.
Everyone thought your father wonderful
And so did I, until I married him
And knew him for a shell: James is like him.
He cannot live an hour without applause.
No one can say that I have stinted it.
But you, you were to be the truly strong
Who must be kept from all that could infect
Or weaken; it was for you I steeled my love
Deliberately and hid it. Do you think that it was
     easy
To shut you out? I who yearned to make
My heart the cosiest nook in all the world
And warm you there for ever, so to leave you
Stark to the indifferent blizzard and the lightning?
How many nights have I not bit my pillow
As the temptation fought to pick you out of bed
And cover you with kisses? But I won.
You were to be unlike your father and your brother
You were to have the power to stand alone;
And to withhold from loving must be all my love.
I won, I said—but was the victory real?
There was a mother crucified herself
To save her favourite son from weakness,
Unlike his twin, his brother who depended

Upon the constant praises of the little.
She saved him nothing: he must have them too
Because his brother had them. She had died
To make him free; but when the moment came
To choose the greatest action of his life
He could not do it, for his brother asked him
And he was padlocked to a brother's hatred——
RANSOM. Mother, stop!
MOTHER. 　　　　　　Michael! You mean——?
RANSOM. Yes. Go to James and tell him that you won.
And may it give him pleasure.
MOTHER. My boy!
　　　　[*She attempts to embrace him. He turns away.*]
　　　　　　　　BLACK OUT
　　　　[*Music. The darkness is filled with* VOICES *of*
　　　　NEWSBOYS, *screaming like cats.*]
Evening Special! Evening Special!
Ransom to lead Expedition!
Famous Climber's Decision!
Evening Moon: Late Night Final!
Young English Climber's Daredevil Attempt!
The Haunted Mountain: Full Story and Pictures!
Monasteries in Sudoland: Amazing Revelations!
　　　　[*The* STAGE-BOX *on the right is illuminated.*
　　　　MRS A. *is reading a morning paper.*]
MRS A. I read the papers; there is nothing there
But news of failure and despair:
The savage train-wreck in the dead of night,
The fire in the school, the children caught alight,
The starving actor in the oven lying,

48

The cashier shot in the grab-raid and left dying,
The young girl slain upon the surgeon's table,
The poison-bottle with the harmless label,
The workman fallen in the scalding vat,
The father's strained heart stopping as he sat,
The student driven crazy by his reading,
The roadside accident hopelessly bleeding,
The bankrupt quaking at the postman's knock,
The moaning murderer baited in the dock——

　　　　[*Enter* MR A. *with evening paper.*]

MR A.　Look, Mary! Read this!
　　　　[*As they read,* VOICES *are heard from the dark-*
　　　　ness of the stage.]

VOICES.　Michael Forsyth Ransom.
　　Eight stone six. Aged twenty-eight years.
　　Short and blue-eyed.
　　His first experiences the rectory elms and the gar-
　　　　den quarry.
　　Kept a tame rook. Was privately educated,
　　By a Hungarian tutor.
　　Climbed the west buttress of Clogwyn Du'r Arddu
　　While still in his teens. The late Colonel Bow said:
　　'That boy will go far.'
　　Visited Switzerland; in a single season
　　Made a new traverse on the Grandes Jorasses,
　　Did the Furggen Shoulder and the Green Needle of
　　　　Chamonix.
　　Studied physiology in Vienna under Niedermeyer.
　　Went to the Julian Alps,
　　Conquered Triglav, mastered the Scarlet Crag.

D　　　　　　　49

Disappeared into Asia Minor, appeared in the
    Caucasus
On two-headed Ushba, returned to England,
In an old windmill near the mouth of the Nen
Translated Confucius during a summer.
Is unmarried. Hates dogs. Plays the viola da gamba.
Is said to be an authority on Goya.
Drinks and eats little but is fond of crystallized
    apricots. . . .

    [*The* STAGE-BOX *on the left is illuminated.*
LORD STAGMANTLE *is seen at the microphone.*]

STAGMANTLE. It goes without saying that the other
members of the Expedition are the finest flower of
English Mountaineering; and, in hands as capable
and brilliant as these, the honour and prestige of
Britain, may, I am sure, be safely left. In this
machine-ridden age, some people are tempted to
suppose that Adventure is dead; but the spirit of
Man has never refused to respond to the challenge
of the unknown and men will always be found ready
to take up the gauntlet, mindless of worldly profit,
undaunted by hardship and risk, unheeding the
dull spirit which can only sneer: Cui bono? From
such pioneers, the man in the street may learn to
play his part in the great game of life, small though
it may be, with a keener zest and daring—— [*Exit.*]

    [*Meanwhile, the* A.'s *have been cutting photo-
graphs and articles out of the paper and pinning
them to the walls of the box.*]

MR A. Cut out the photos and pin them to the wall,

Cut out the map and follow the details of it all,
Follow the progress of this mountain mission,
Day by day let it inspire our lowly condition.

MRS A.

Many have come to us often with their conscious
    charms,
They stood upon platforms and madly waved their
    arms,
At the top of their voices they promised all we lack,
They offered us glory but they wanted it back.

MR A.

But these are prepared to risk their lives in action
In which the peril is their only satisfaction.
They have not asked us to alter our lives
Or to eat less meat or to be more kind to our wives.

    [LADY ISABEL *appears at the microphone in the*
    STAGE-BOX, *L.*]

ISABEL. The Englishman is reserved. He does not wear
his heart on his sleeve nor put his best goods in his
shop-window. He smokes his pipe and answers in
words of one syllable. So that those who do not
know him think that he is stupid and cold. But
every now and then, now in this part of the world,
now in that, something generous, something brave
or beautiful, just happens. And when we start to
investigate it we shall generally find that, at the
bottom of it all, is an Englishman. I have had the
privilege of meeting Mr Ransom and his companions on this expedition personally; and I can say
with absolute sincerity that never in my life have I

come away feeling so exalted, so proud that I belonged to the same country and the same race as these gallant men. . . . [*Exit.*]

MRS A. They make no promise to improve our station,
At our weakness they make no show of indignation,
They do not offer contemptuously to lend a hand
But their courage is something the least can understand.

MR A. The corner tobacconist and the booking-clerk,
The naked miner hewing in the dark,
The forge-hand sweating at the huge steam-hammer,
The girl imprisoned in the tower of a stammer——

MRS A. The invalid, sheep-counting all the night,
The small, the tall, the black-haired and the white
See something each can estimate,
They can read of these actions and know them great.
[GUNN *appears at the microphone in the* STAGE-BOX, *left.*]

GUNN. I don't really know exactly what to say. We none of us know what F 6 is going to be like. If you ask me, I think she's probably an ugly old maid. I'm scared stiff, but Ransom will hold our hands, I expect. . . . We shall be a jolly party; at least, I hope so. I've been on one or two of these expeditions and no one's murdered me yet. They say that there's a ghost at the top; but I've made Doctor Williams promise that if we see anything he'll let me hide behind him. Well, I don't think I've got anything else to say, so I'll tell you a limerick I've just made up:

52

There was an old man of F 6
Who had some extraordinary tricks:
He took off——

[*An* ANNOUNCER *comes hastily into the* BOX, *pushes* GUNN *aside and speaks into the microphone.*]

ANNOUNCER. We are all most grateful to Mr Gunn for his very interesting talk. Listeners will no doubt join us in wishing the party every success. There will now be a short interval in the programme.

[*Exit* BOTH. STAGE-BOX, *left, is darkened.*]

MRS A. John, I'm so happy! Can't we do something to celebrate?

MR A. Let's go away for the week-end. Let's go now!

MRS A. But it's seven o'clock and supper's nearly ready!

MR A. O, bother the supper! Let it burn!

MRS A. Let's go away and never return;
Catch the last train to——

MR A. Where to?

MRS A. What does it matter?
Anywhere out of this rush and this clatter!
Get your toothbrush, get your pyjamas,
Fetch your razor and let us be gone,
Hurry and pack, may we never come back;
For Youth goes quickly and Age comes on!
[THEY *begin to put on their outdoor clothes, pack, etc.*]

MR A. Dover would like us, Margate would welcome us,

53

Hastings and Folkestone would give us a part,
Hove be excited and Brighton delighted,
Southend would take us warm to her heart.

BOTH. Moments of happiness do not come often,
Opportunity's easy to miss.
O, let us seize them, of all their joy squeeze them,
For Monday returns when none may kiss!

[*Exeunt.*]

[*After the A's have departed for Hove, the stage boxes are darkened. A sudden penumbra of light on the stage shows* MRS RANSOM *seated in a high-backed chair facing the audience.*]

MRS RANSOM [*talking to herself in a hoarse and penetrating whisper*]. Michael . . . Michael darling . . . can you hear me? There, there. . . . It's all right. . . . There's nothing to be frightened about. Mother's with you. Of course she won't leave you alone, Michael, never. Wherever you are, whatever you're doing, whether you know it or not, she's near you with her love; for you belong to her always. She's with you now, at sea, on board the ship with your foolish companions, and she'll be with you on the mountain, too. . . . Of course you'll get to the top, darling. Mother will help you. She'll always help you. Wasn't she with you from the very beginning, when you were a tiny baby? Of course she was! And she'll be with you at the very end. . . .

RANSOM [*voice heard, very far off, frightened*]. It's the Demon, mother!

54

MRS RANSOM [*sings*]. Michael, you shall be renowned,
    When the Demon you have drowned,
    A cathedral we will build
    When the Demon you have killed.
    When the Demon is dead,
    You shall have a lovely clean bed.

    You shall be mine, all mine,
    You shall have kisses like wine,
    When the wine gets into your head
    Mother will see that you're not misled;
    A saint am I and a saint are you
    It's perfectly, perfectly, perfectly true.

BLACK OUT

END OF ACT I

ACT II

ACT II

SCENE I

[*F* 6. *Room in a Monastery on the Great Glacier. A high, gloomy, vaulted chamber, with doors L. into the courtyard and R. into the interior of the building. In the back wall, arches open into a cloister, beyond which the greenish, faintly glowing ice of the glacier is visible.*]

> [MICHAEL RANSOM *and* SHAWCROSS *are seated at a table in the foreground, on which stand three silver candlesticks with church candles of coloured wax.* RANSOM *and* SHAWCROSS *both have notebooks and pencils; they are checking stores.*]

RANSOM. How many tins of malted milk?

SHAWCROSS. Fifty.

RANSOM. How are we off for pemmican?

SHAWCROSS. Three two-pound tins.

RANSOM. We must remember to ask the monks for yak butter. . . . How about the petrol for the primus?

SHAWCROSS. God, that reminds me! [*He jumps up and goes to the door L. Looks out into the courtyard.*] Two porters haven't finished unloading it yet! [*Shouts.*]

Hi! Sing ko, pan no ah! Teng fang! Naga! Naga!
[*Returns to table.*] Lazy devils! And it'll be dark in a
few minutes.... That's what comes of leaving things
to Gunn. He treats this whole business like a picnic.

[*He glances quickly at* RANSOM, *who does not,
however, respond.*]

RANSOM. Have we got enough soup cubes?

SHAWCROSS. Three large packets. [*Hesitates.*] Look
here, M. F., I've been wanting to talk to you about
Gunn for a long time now. . . . You know, I hate to
bother you with this sort of thing. . . . I've tried to
keep you from noticing . . .

RANSOM [*smiles*]. Have you?

SHAWCROSS. You mean, you *did* see something? Well,
in a way, I'm glad. Because, if you hadn't, you
mightn't have believed me——

RANSOM. I saw that Gunn teased the yaks and scared
the porters and played tricks on Tom and Teddy—
and on you, too, Ian. I agree that he's often an intolerable nuisance; and I think that without him
this expedition would be much more businesslike
and very gloomy indeed.

SHAWCROSS [*exasperated*]. The thing I admire most
about you, M. F., is your wonderful broadminded-
ness. It's an example to me. I'm not very tolerant,
I'm afraid. If Gunn amused you and the others, I'm
glad. I hope I can see a joke as well as anyone. . . . But
that wasn't quite what I meant, just now. This
is something quite different. I hardly like to tell
you——

Ransom. If you hadn't meant to tell me, Ian, you wouldn't have started this conversation at all.

Shawcross [*blurting it out*]. Well then—Gunn steals!

Ransom [*laughs*]. Oh, that!

Shawcross. So you *did* know!

Ransom. I'm surprised that you've only just noticed it. He steals like a magpie; bits of indiarubber, chiefly, but also watches, pencils, and, occasionally, money. . . . That reminds me, I expect he's taken my camera. I was imagining I'd lost it down in the gorge, while we were fording the river.

Shawcross. But, M. F., you can't tolerate this kind of thing! What are you going to do?

Ransom. Ask him if he's got it.

Shawcross. But surely there's more to it than that? How can you take a man with you who's just a common thief? One has to have some standards of decency, I suppose?

Ransom [*smiles*]. You haven't changed much, have you, Ian, since you were captain of your school?

Shawcross [*bitterly*]. You're always laughing at me. I suppose you think I'm just a priggish fool?

Ransom. I certainly don't think you're a fool. You know that I rely on your help more than anybody's to make this expedition a success.

Shawcross. Thank you, M. F. You make me feel ashamed. As long as you trust me, then I don't give a damn what anybody else says or thinks. You know I'd follow you anywhere. We all would. . . . The wonderful thing about a man like you is that

61

you can use all kinds of people and get the best out of each. I think I understand better, now, what it is you get out of Gunn. I don't want to run him down —just because his brand of humour's a bit too subtle for me. [*With increasing bitterness.*] He's not a bad sort in his way; he's all right to have about the place, I suppose, as long as there's no special difficulty or danger. He's a damn good climber, too, I admit—only he simply hasn't got the temperament. I'm wondering what he'll be like up there, on the north face. You remember how he screamed, that day in the Coolins, and wouldn't budge for an hour? It was pitiful.

RANSOM. David's always frightened when he climbs. Otherwise, he wouldn't climb. Being frightened is his chief pleasure in life. He's frightened when he drives a racing-car or seduces somebody's wife. At present he prefers mountaineering because it frightens him most of all.

SHAWCROSS. How well you understand him, M. F.! Now, that's just the point I wanted to make: wouldn't it be better, when we get to Camp A, to leave Gunn behind?

RANSOM [*smiles*]. To damage all the instruments and eat up all the stores?

SHAWCROSS. Well, but, I mean, he'll have to be dropped somewhere, won't he? [*Pause.*] Do you really think it's wise to take him as far as Camp B?

RANSOM. I shall decide when the time comes.

62

SHAWCROSS. I mean, it's quite settled, isn't it, that only two of us shall try to reach the summit?

RANSOM. Yes. There'll be only two of us.

SHAWCROSS. And you can't, for a moment, be thinking of taking Gunn? [*Pause.*] My God, it'd be madness! M. F.—you couldn't!

RANSOM. Have I said I shall?

SHAWCROSS [*with growing excitement*]. If I thought such a thing was possible, I'd—I don't know what I'd do! Gunn, that miserable little rotter! Why, he's not a climber at all! He's just a neurotic! He poses. He does everything for effect! Just a beastly little posing coward! [*Pause.*] Oh, I know you think I'm simply jealous!

[*Enter* LAMP *and the* DOCTOR, *L.*]

LAMP [*excited*]. The flora here is amazing, simply amazing! I've had one of the most wonderful afternoons of my life! I tell you what, Doctor——[*Sees the others.*] Oh, here you are, M. F.! Didn't see you in the dark.

[SHAWCROSS *silently lights the candles.*]

I was just telling the Doctor, I've had a field-day! Extraordinarily interesting! M. F., I'm convinced that Hawkins is wrong when he denies the possibility of a five-leaved Polus Naufrangia! And what's more, I don't mind betting you I shall find one here, on F 6.

RANSOM. Let's see what you got this afternoon.

LAMP [*opens his vasculum*]. Here's Stagnium Menengitis and Frustrax Abominum.... Isn't it a beauty!

63

And look here, here's something to surprise you: you told me there wasn't a Rossus Monstrens with blue petals! Well, what do you say to this?

RANSOM [*examines flower*]. This is interesting.

[*Enter* GUNN. *L.*]

GUNN. Ah, here you all are! Thank goodness! I've been hunting for you everywhere! I began to think something had happened to you. . . . [*Sits down and mops his forehead.*]

DOCTOR. What's the matter with you, David? You look rattled.

GUNN. You'd be rattled if you'd been hanging round this place all the afternoon. Ugh! It gives me the creeps!

DOCTOR. Why, what's wrong with it?

GUNN. Those beastly monks. . . . Don't they make you feel damned queer, with those cowls over their faces? I've been watching them for hours, out there: they never seem to speak or make any signs; they just stand facing each other, like this—and yet you have a nasty sort of feeling that they're talking, somehow. . . . I shouldn't wonder if they do it by telepathy or something.

DOCTOR. They seemed quite friendly and harmless when we arrived.

GUNN. Don't you believe it. . . . They're plotting to do us in while we're asleep, I bet you they are. . . . This afternoon, when I was sitting watching the porters unload, I kept imagining there was somebody standing just behind me. Several times I turned round quickly to try and catch him, but

64

there was nothing there. . . . And then I saw a monk and I thought I'd ask him which room we could use for the stores. So I went over to him and made signs and he seemed to understand all right. He turned round and went to one of the doors and opened it and went inside. Naturally, I followed him. But when I got into the room, there was nobody there. And there wasn't even a window he could have got out of. . . . No, I don't like this place!

DOCTOR. I tell you what, David, you've had a touch of the sun. I'll give you something to make you sleep well tonight.

RANSOM. Oh, by the way, David, where's my camera? You've got it, haven't you?

GUNN [*with a charming smile*]. Yes. It's in my room. I thought I'd look after it for you for a bit.

SHAWCROSS. Well, of all the blasted——!

RANSOM. That was very kind of you. Would you bring it here now, please?

GUNN. Very well—if you'd rather——

[*As he moves towards the door, L., a low chanting begins from the courtyard outside. This chant continues throughout the following scene. Its words are:*]

Go Ga, morum tonga tara
Mi no tang hum valka vara
So so so kum mooni lara

Korkra ha Chormopuloda
Antifora lampisoda
Kang ku gar, bari baroda

Ming ting ishta sokloskaya
No rum ga ga, no rum gaya
Nong Chormopuloda sya.

GUNN. My God! What's that? [*Retreats hastily behind* RANSOM'S *chair.*]

SHAWCROSS [*goes to door L. and looks out*]. They're all gathered out there in the courtyard. They're starting a procession. Now they're beginning to go round in circles. They've got torches and banners. . . .

GUNN. Lock that door, for Heaven's sake! Suppose they come in here!

SHAWCROSS. Do you ever think of anything except your own beastly little skin?

[*Meanwhile the others have joined him at the door.* GUNN *comes last, unwillingly, curious in spite of himself.*]

DOCTOR. From the way they walk it might be a funeral.

LAMP. I believe it *is* a funeral. Look what they're carrying.

GUNN. A coffin! Gosh, did you see?

DOCTOR. Cheer up, David; there's only one! Perhaps they won't choose you.

GUNN. It's most likely some wretched traveller they've murdered.

DOCTOR. Very curious, those masks. A pity it's too dark for a photograph.

SHAWCROSS. Now they're going. I wonder where that door leads to? Probably into the temple precincts.

[*The chanting dies away.*]

66

LAMP [*as they close the door and return downstage to the table*]. What did you make of it, M. F.?

RANSOM. I've read about these rites, somewhere. They're supposed to propitiate the spirits which guard the house of the dead.

GUNN. Anyhow, I hope there won't be any more! Phew! This place is about as cheerful as Woking Cemetery!

> [*As he speaks, the door on the R. opens noiselessly and a cowled* MONK *enters, carrying in his hands a crystal which glows faintly with a bluish light.*]

You chaps didn't really think I was scared, did you? I was only ragging. It takes more than a few old monks to frighten *me*! [*Turns and suddenly sees the* MONK. *Screams.*] Oh, God!

> [*As the* MONK *advances towards the front of the stage,* GUNN *retreats backwards before him.*]

What does he want? Help! Do something, somebody! M. F., you speak to him!

RANSOM. Om no hum, no na num se? [*Pause.*] No num seng ka, gang se gang? [*Pause.*] King t'sang po, ka no ah? [*Pause.*] Either he doesn't understand any of the three hill-dialects, or he isn't allowed to answer.

DOCTOR. Funny kind of a lamp he's got there. [*Approaches.*]

GUNN. I say! Do be careful! He may have a knife up his sleeve!

DOCTOR. Extraordinary thing—it doesn't seem to be a

lamp at all. It just shines. [*Bends over the crystal.*]
Why, it's a kind of mirror—I can see myself in it!
Am I really as fat as that? Gracious, I'm quite bald!
Hullo, what's this? I'm sitting in an armchair. I
seem to know that room. . . . Yes, it's the Reform
Club! I say, I think I must have got a touch of the
sun like David. Am I just seeing things? Here,
Teddy, you come and look!

LAMP [*looks*]. Polus Naufrangia! As plain as anything:
all five leaves. By Jove, what a beauty! [*Rubs his
eyes.*] I must be going mad!

GUNN. He's hypnotizing you, that's what it is! When
we're all in a trance, we shall probably be murdered. . . . I say, I must have a look!

LAMP [*excited*]. I saw it as plain as that candle! Five
distinct leaves!

GUNN [*looks*]. Why, there's my old Alfa Romeo! And
someone's sitting in it—it's a woman, dressed all in
black! She seems to be at a cross-roads. I see the
sign-post, but I can't read what's written on it. . . .
Now she's turning her head. My God, it's Toni—
Mrs da Silva! [*Comes away.*] Do you think that
means her husband's died and now she'll follow me
out here? Come on, Ian. Your turn!

SHAWCROSS [*takes a pace towards the crystal, stops,
bursts out violently*]. I'm not going to have anything
to do with this damned business! You others please
yourselves. It isn't right. We aren't meant to know
these things. [*Calmer.*] It's probably some kind of
trick, anyhow. . . . M. F., I'm going to get the

wireless ready. It's nearly time to pick up the weather report from Fort George. [*Takes up one of the candles and exits, L.*]

GUNN. You'll have a look, won't you, M. F.?

RANSOM [*hesitates a moment*]. Very well. [*Looks into crystal.*]

> [*As he does so, voices are heard from the darkened stage-boxes.*]

VOICES. Give me bread

> Restore my dead

I am sick

> Help me quick

Give me a car

> Make me a star

Make me neat

> Guide my feet

Make me strong

> Teach me where I belong

Strengthen my will

> Make me still

Make me admired

> Make me desired

Make me just

> Cool my lust.

[*Together*].

> Make us kind
> Make us of one mind
> Make us brave
> > Save
> > Save
> > Save
> > Save.

DOCTOR. Well, what is it this time? Motors or flowers or London clubs?

69

GUNN. Try and see something useful. Ask it to tell you the best route up F 6.

RANSOM [*after a long pause*]. I can see nothing.

GUNN. Nothing at all? Oh, M. F.!

DOCTOR. That all goes to support your hypnotism theory. M. F. was a bit too strong for him.

[*The* MONK *turns silently and goes out by the door, R.*]

GUNN. Ought we to have tipped him, or anything? Gosh, you know, that crystal has given me quite a headache! I can't understand your not seeing anything, M. F. Or was it so awful that you won't tell us?

DOCTOR. I feel I could do with a change of air. Let's go and see if Ian's got Fort George.

GUNN. Right you are. Coming, M. F.?

RANSOM. No. I'll stay here. The Abbot may wish to speak to me.

[GUNN *and* DOCTOR *go out, L.*]

RANSOM. Bring back the crystal. Let me look again and prove my vision a poor fake. Was it to me they turned their rodent faces, those ragged denizens of the waterfronts, and squealed so piteously: 'Restore us! Restore us to our uniqueness and our human condition.' Was it for me the prayer of the sad artist on the crowded beaches was indeed intended? 'Assassinate my horrible detachment. My love for these bathers is hopeless and excessive. Make me also a servant.' I thought I saw the raddled sick cheeks of the world light up at my approach as

70

at the home-coming of an only son. . . . How could I tell them that?

> [*Enter the* ABBOT *and* TWO ACOLYTES, *R.*]

ABBOT [*makes sign of benediction*]. Only God is great.

RANSOM [*kneels and kisses his hand*]. But His power is for mercy.

ABBOT. I hope everything has been arranged to your satisfaction?

RANSOM. It is perfect.

ABBOT. I am glad. Please be seated, Mr Ransom. Will you do me the honour of taking a glass of wine with me? In these mountains, I fear we can offer but poor hospitality, but I think you will not find this wine totally unworthy of your palate. Your health, Mr Ransom.

> [*Toast.*]

> [*The* ACOLYTES *exeunt R.*]

Now tell me. You wish to start soon on your ascension of our mountain?

RANSOM. Tomorrow. If He permit it, Whose will must be done.

ABBOT. You know the legend?

RANSOM. I have read the Book of the Dead.

ABBOT. Such interest, Mr Ransom, is uncommon in one of your race. In that case, you will have comprehended the meaning of the ceremony that was performed this evening out in the courtyard: the office for the souls of the dead and the placation of the Demon. I am afraid that you, with your western civilization, must consider us here excessively

71

superstitious. . . . No, you need not contradict me out of politeness. I understand. You see the painted mask and the horns and the eyes of fire and you think: 'This Demon is only a bogey that nurses use to frighten their children: I have outgrown such nonsense. It is fit only for ignorant monks and peasants. With our factory chimneys and our furnaces and our locomotives we have banished these fairy-tales. I shall climb the mountain and I shall see nothing.' But you would be wrong. The peasants, as you surmise rightly, are simple and uneducated; so their vision is simple and uneducated. They see the truth as a crude and coloured picture. Perhaps, for that reason, they see it more clearly than you or I. For it is a picture of truth. The Demon is real. Only his ministry and his visitation are unique for every nature. To the complicated and sensitive like yourself, Mr Ransom, his disguises are more subtle. He is—what shall I say?—the formless terror in the dream, the stooping shadow that withdraws itself as you wake in the half-dawn. You have heard his gnashing accusations in the high fever at a very great distance. You have felt his presence in the sinister contours of a valley or the sudden hostility of a copse or the choking apprehension that fills you unaccountably in the middle of the most intimate dinner-party. I did you an injustice just now when I said that you expected to see nothing on the mountain. You do expect to see something. That is why you are intending to climb it. You do not make that foolish, that terrible mistake so common among your fellow-countrymen of imagining that it is fortunate to be alive. No. You know, as I do, that Life is evil. You have conquered the first temptation of the Demon, which is to blind Man to his existence. But that victory exposes you to a second and infinitely more dangerous temptation; the temptation of pity; the temptation to overcome the Demon by will. Mr Ransom, I think I understand your temptation. You wish to conquer the Demon and then to save mankind. Am I right?

RANSOM. So you know of my vision in the crystal?

ABBOT. Ah, you saw it there, too? That is not strange. For all men see reflected there some fragment of their nature and glimpse a knowledge of those forces by whose free operation the future is forecast and limited. That is not supernatural. Nothing is revealed but what we have hidden from ourselves; the treasure we have buried and accursed. Your temptation, Mr Ransom, is written in your face. You know your powers and your intelligence. You could ask the world to follow you and it would serve you with blind obedience; for most men long to be delivered from the terror of thinking and feeling for themselves. And yours is the nature to which those are always attracted in whom the desire for devotion and self-immolation is strongest. And you would do them much good. Because men desire evil, they must be governed by those who under-

stand the corruption of their hearts, and can set
bounds to it. As long as the world endures, there
must be order, there must be government: but woe
to the governors, for, by the very operation of
their duty, however excellent, they themselves are
destroyed. For you can only rule men by appealing
to their fear and their lust; government requires the
exercise of the human will: and the human will is
from the Demon.

RANSOM. Supposing you are right. Supposing I aban-
don the mountain. What shall I do? Return to
England and become a farm labourer or a factory
hand?

ABBOT. You have gone too far for that.

RANSOM. Well then——

ABBOT. There is an alternative, Mr Ransom; and I
offer it you.

RANSOM. What?

ABBOT. To remain here and make the complete abne-
gation of the will.

RANSOM. And that means——?

ABBOT. You saw the corpse in the procession?

RANSOM. Yes.

ABBOT. In the course of your studies you have become
acquainted, no doubt, with the mysteries of the
rites of Chöd? The celebrant withdraws to a wild
and lonely spot and there the corpse is divided and
its limbs scattered. The celebrant, sounding on his
bone trumpet, summons the gluttonous demons of
the air to their appointed feast. At this moment

74

there issues from the crown of his head a terrible goddess. This goddess is his Will, and she is armed with a sword. And as the ghouls of the mountain and of the sky and of the waters under the glacier assemble to partake of the banquet, the goddess with her sword cuts off the limbs of the celebrant's esoteric body, scatters them and apportions his entrails among the demon guests. And the celebrant must wish them good appetite, urging them to devour every morsel. These rites, Mr Ransom, are so terrible that frequently the novices who witness them foam at the mouth, or become unconscious or fall dead where they stand. And yet, so tedious is the path that leads us to perfection that, when all these rites have been accomplished, the process of self surrender can hardly be said to have begun. . . . Well, Mr Ransom, I must leave you now. Do not make up your mind at once. Think my proposal over.

RANSOM. Before you go, may I ask you a question? As Abbot, you rule this monastery?

ABBOT. That is a wise observation. Mr Ransom, I am going to tell you a secret which I have never told a living soul. We have spoken of your temptation. I am now going to tell you of mine. Sometimes, when I am tired or ill, I am subject to very strange attacks. They come without warning, in the middle of the night, in the noon siesta, even during the observance of the most sacred religious rites. Sometimes they come frequently, sometimes they

75

do not occur for months or even years at a time. When they come I am filled with an intoxicating excitement, so that my hand trembles and all the hairs on my body bristle, and there comes suddenly into my mind strange words, snatches of song and even whole poems. These poems sing always of the same world. A strange world. The world of the common people. The world of blood and violent death, of peasant soldiers and murderers, of graves and disappointed lust. And when I come to myself again and see these monastery walls around me, I am filled with horror and despair. For I know that it is a visitation of the Demon. I know that, for me, nothing matters any more: it is too late. I am already among the lost. Good-night, Mr Ransom.

[*Exit R.*]

RANSOM. Is it too late for me? I recognize my purpose. There was a choice once, in the Lakeland Inn. I made it wrong; and if I choose again now, I must choose for myself alone, not for these others. Oh, You who are the history and the creator of all these forms in which we are condemned to suffer, to whom the necessary is also the just, show me, show each of us upon this mortal star the danger that under His hand is softly palpitating. Save us, save us from the destructive element of our will, for all we do is evil.

[*Enter* GUNN, *L.*]

GUNN. You alone? Good. I was afraid I might be butting in; but Ian and the others threw me out.

And I didn't much like the idea of sitting by myself in the dark, with all those monks around. [*Pause.*] Are you busy, M. F.? Would you rather I didn't talk?

[RANSOM *is deep in his thoughts. He doesn't answer.* GUNN, *after regarding him for a moment in silence, begins again.*]

The wireless is coming through beautifully. No atmospherics at all. I heard the weather report; first class. We'll be able to start tomorrow for a cert.

RANSOM. You sound pleased.

GUNN. Of course I'm pleased! Who wouldn't be—after all these weeks of messing about? Tomorrow we shall be on the ice!

RANSOM. Tell me, David; what is it that makes you so keen to climb this mountain?

GUNN [*laughs*]. What is it that makes one keen to climb any mountain?

RANSOM. F 6 is not like any mountain you have ever climbed.

GUNN. Why not? It's got a top, hasn't it? And we want to get to it, don't we? I don't see anything very unusual in that.

RANSOM. You've thought enough about the ascent of F 6 no doubt; about the couloirs and the north buttress and the arête. . . . Have you thought about the descent, too: the descent that goes down and down into the place where Stagmantle and my Brother and all their gang are waiting? Have you thought about the crowds in the streets down there, and the loudspeakers and the posing and the photographing and the hack-written articles you'll be paid thousands to sign? Have you smelt the smell of their ceremonial banquets? Have you loathed them, and even as you were loathing them, begun to like it all? [*Becomes hysterically excited.*] Have you? Have you?

GUNN [*scared*]. M. F., what on earth do you mean?

RANSOM. Don't lie to me now, David. Are you corrupt, like the rest of us? I must know. [*Seizes* GUNN *by the wrists and stares into his face.*] Yes. Yes. I see it! You too. How horrible! [*Throws him violently aside.*] Get out of my sight!

    [*Enter* SHAWCROSS, DOCTOR *and* LAMP; *all far too excited to notice that anything unusual has been happening.*]

SHAWCROSS. M. F.! A message has just come through: Blavek and his party are on the mountain already!

GUNN. But it's impossible! When we last heard, he was still on the other side of the Tung Desert!

SHAWCROSS. Well, this is official. He must have been making forced marches. These fellows aren't mountaineers at all—they're soldiers! There's a whole regiment of them! Do you know, M. F., what they're doing? They're hammering the whole south face full of pitons and hauling each other up like sacks! Good God, they'll be using fire-escapes before they've finished! Well, that settles it! We haven't a moment to lose!

78

RANSOM. And you are all anxious to play their game: the race to the summit? This won't be mountaineering. It'll be a steeplechase. Are you so sure the prize is worth it? Ian, you're the purist: is this your idea of climbing? No time for observations; no time for reconnoitre. Teddy, hadn't you better stay out of this? We can't wait a week, you know, while you look for your flowers.

LAMP. I'll take my chance of that later. We've got to beat Blavek!

RANSOM. Blavek is only another victim of the mountain. And you, Tom?

DOCTOR. You don't expect me to stay here, do you, M. F.? Why, this makes me feel twenty years younger already!

RANSOM. You, too. . . . Stagmantle's latest convert. He should be honoured.

SHAWCROSS. What's the point of all this talk? The people in England expect us to get to the top before the Ostnians. They believe in us. Are we going to let them down?

GUNN. I think this makes it all the more exciting. Good old Blavek!

RANSOM. Very well then, since you wish it. I obey you. The summit will be reached, the Ostnians defeated, the Empire saved. And I have failed. We start at dawn. . . .

CURTAIN

79

[*The* STAGE-BOX *on the right is illuminated.*
The A.'s *are having breakfast.*]

MRS A. Give me some money before you go
There are a number of bills we owe
And you can go to the bank today
During the lunch-hour.

MR A.   I dare say;
But, as it happens, I'm overdrawn.

MRS A. Overdrawn? What on earth have you done
With all the money? Where's it gone?

MR A. How does money always go?
Papers, lunches, tube-fares, teas,
Tooth-paste, stamps and doctor's fees,
Our trip to Hove cost a bit, you know.

MRS A. Can we never have fun? Can we never have any
And not have to count every single penny?
Why can't you find a way to earn more?
It's so degrading and dull to be poor.
Get another job.

MR A.   My job may be small
But I'm damned lucky to have one at all.
When I think of those I knew in the War,
All the fellows about my age:
How many are earning a decent wage?

80

There was O'Shea, the middle-weight cham-
   pion; slouches from bar to bar now in a
   battered hat, cadging for drinks;
There was Morgan, famous for his stories; sells
   ladies' underwear from door to door;
There was Polewhele, with his university education; now Dan the Lavatory Man at a
   third-rate night-club;
And Holmes in our office, well past fifty, was dis-
   missed last week to bring down expenses;
Next week another: who shall it be?
It may be anyone. It may be me.
[*A newspaper is dropped through the door into
the back of the Box. MR A. goes to fetch it.*]

MRS A. It's all this foreign competition:
Czechoslovakia, Russia, Japan,
Ostnia and Westland do all they can
To ruin our trade with their cheap goods,
Dumping them on our market in floods.
It makes my blood boil! You can find
No British goods of any kind
In any of the big shops now.
The Government ought to stop it somehow——

MR A. Listen to this. [*Reads.*] Our Special Correspon-
dent reports that the Ostnian Expedition to F 6,
headed by Blavek, has crossed the Tung Desert and
is about to commence its final assault on the mountain. Blavek is confident of success and, in mountaineering circles, it is believed that the British
climbers will have to make very strenuous efforts

indeed if they are to beat their formidable opponents. . . .

MRS A. You see? The foreigner everywhere,
Competing in trade, competing in sport,
Competing in science and abstract thought:
And we just sit down and let them take
The prizes! There's more than a mountain at
stake.

MR A. The travelogue showed us a Babylon buried in
sand.

MRS A. And books have spoken of a Spain that was the
brilliant centre of an Empire.

MR A. I have found a spider in the opulent board-
room.

MRS A. I have dreamed of a threadbare barnstorming
actor, and he was a national symbol.

MR A. England's honour is covered with rust.

MRS A. Ransom must beat them! He must! He must!

MR A. Or England falls. She has had her hour
And now must decline to a second-class power.
[*Puts on his bowler hat and exit, brandishing his
newspaper. The* STAGE-BOX *is darkened.*]

82

ACT II

SCENE II

[*On F 6. At the foot of the West Buttress. The back of the stage rises slightly, suggesting a precipice beyond. A magnificent panorama of distant mountains. On the right of the stage, the wall of the buttress rises, with an overhang.*]

       [*Midday.* RANSOM, SHAWCROSS *and* LAMP *stand roped on the edge of the precipice, assisting the* DOCTOR *and* GUNN, *who are still out of sight, below. The rope is belayed round a rock.*]

RANSOM [*looking down*]. There's a hold to your left, Tom. No, a little higher up. Good. Now you're all right.

GUNN'S VOICE [*from below*]. Look out, Doc.! Don't tread on my face!

RANSOM. Now then. . . .

       [*After a moment, the* DOCTOR *hoists himself into view, panting.*]

Now you take it easy, Tom. Fifteen minutes' rest, here.

LAMP. We've made good time, this morning.

RANSOM [*looking down*]. You all right, David?

Gunn's Voice [*from below*]. I think so. . . . No! Ooh, er! Gosh, this rock is soft! Here we come!

[*He appears.*]

Doctor. Well, thank goodness, that couloir's behind us, anyhow. Though how we shall ever get down it again is another matter.

Ransom. You were splendid, Tom. Never known you in better form.

Doctor. I must have lost at least two stone. That's one comfort.

Gunn. While we were in the chimney, I felt his sweat dripping on to me like a shower-bath. . . . I say, isn't there anything more to eat?

Ransom. I'm afraid we must keep to our rations, David. We're only carrying the minimum, you know.

Shawcross. I should have thought you'd eaten enough to satisfy even *your* appetite—considering you had all my chocolate, as well.

Gunn. Well, you needn't make a grievance out of it. You didn't want it, did you?

Doctor. Still feeling sick, Ian?

Shawcross [*crossly*]. I'm all right.

Doctor. You don't look any too good.

Shawcross. Anyhow, I don't see that it helps much to keep fussing about trifles and thinking of one's comfort.

[*A pause.*]

Lamp. Well, if we've got another ten minutes to spare, I think I'll be taking a look round. Might spot a

84

clump of Polus Naufrangia. You never know. It's
about the right altitude, now.

[*He goes to the back of the stage and looks over,
through his binoculars.*]

GUNN [*following him*]. See anything?

[LAMP *shakes his head.*]

Gosh, that's a drop! [*He balances on the edge and
pretends to wobble.*] Ooh, er! Help!

RANSOM. Come away from there, David.

[GUNN *obeys and begins wandering about the
stage.*]

DOCTOR [*pointing upwards*]. How high do you make
that buttress?

RANSOM. About seventeen hundred feet. We shall be
on it all this afternoon. We ought to reach the ridge
easily by sunset.

GUNN [*poking about*]. Hullo, what's this? [*Picks up a
skull.*] Doctor Livingstone, I presume?

[*The others, except* LAMP, *who continues to peer
through his binoculars, collect round* GUNN.]

How on earth did he get here?

DOCTOR. Goodness knows. May have fallen from above.
See this crack? It's hardly likely to have been murder, up here.

SHAWCROSS. Anyhow, he must have been a pretty useful climber to have got as far as he did. I suppose
there's no doubt it's a native skull?

DOCTOR. Impossible to say. It may have been some
mad European who thought he'd have a shot
at F 6 on his own; but that's scarcely possible.

85

Some herdsman, probably. . . . What do you think,
M. F.?

[*Hands him the skull.*]

LAMP [*shouting excitedly*]. Come here! Look!

GUNN. What's the matter, Teddy?

LAMP. Polus Naufrangia! Five-leaved! A beauty! Only
just spotted it. And it was right under my nose!

[*He begins lowering himself over the edge.*]

DOCTOR. Wait a moment, Teddy. Better do that on the
rope.

GUNN [*looking over*]. He'll be all right. It's a broad
ledge. Only about twenty feet down.

DOCTOR [*looking over*]. Careful, Teddy. Careful. Take
your time.

LAMP'S VOICE [*from below*]. I'm all right.

[*The others, except* RANSOM, *stand looking over
the edge.*]

RANSOM [*to skull*]. Well, Master; the novices are here.
Have your dry bones no rustle of advice to give
them? Or are you done with climbing? But that's
improbable. Imagination sees the ranges in the
Country of the Dead, where those to whom a mountain is a mother find an eternal playground. There
Antoine de Ville scales pinnacles with subtle en-
gines; Gesner drinks water, shares his dreams with
Saussure, whose passion for Mont Blanc became a
kind of illness. Paccard is reconciled with Balmont,
and Bourrit, the cathedral precentor, no longer fal-
sifies their story. Marie-Coutett still keeps his nick-
name of The Weasel; Donkin and Fox are talking

86

of the Caucasus; Whymper goes climbing with his friends again and Hadow, who made the slip of inexperience, has no faults. While, on the strictest buttresses, the younger shadows look for fresher routes: Toni Schmidt is there and the Bavarian cyclists; and that pair also whom Odell saw on the step of Everest before the cloud hid them for ever, in the gigantic shadow of whose achievement we pitch our miserable tent——

        [*The roar of an approaching avalanche is heard.*]

DOCTOR. An avalanche! My God!

        [RANSOM *runs to join the others.*]

Look out, Teddy! Look out!

GUNN. Quick, man!

SHAWCROSS. Stay where you are!

GUNN. Jump for it!

DOCTOR. Oh, God! He's done for!

        [*The roar of the avalanche drowns their voices; then gradually dies away.*]

SHAWCROSS. He was just stooping to pick the flower, when the first stone got him.

DOCTOR. It was all over in a moment. He was probably knocked right out.

SHAWCROSS. As he went over the edge, you could see the flower in his hand.

GUNN. Gosh, I feel beastly!

        [*Sits down on a rock.*]

SHAWCROSS. He was a damn good man!

DOCTOR. I'm glad he found the Naufrangia, anyway. We must tell them that in London. Perhaps the five-leaved kind will be named after him. He'd like that, I think.

SHAWCROSS. I just can't believe it. Five minutes ago, he was standing here.

DOCTOR [*looking at* LAMP'S *rucksack, which is lying on a rock*]. What do you think we ought to do with this? His people might like to have it.

SHAWCROSS. We can't very well take it with us now. I think we'd better bury it here. We can pick it up on our way down.

DOCTOR. Right you are. I'll help you. [*Begins collecting stones.*]

[SHAWCROSS *picks up the rucksack.*]

GUNN. Poor old Teddy! [*To* SHAWCROSS.] Half a minute! [*Feels in the pocket of the rucksack.*] Oh, good!

[*Pulls out a piece of chocolate and begins eating it.*]

SHAWCROSS [*horrified*]. My God! Haven't you any decency left in you at all?

GUNN [*with his mouth full*]. Why, what's the matter now?

SHAWCROSS. Of all the filthy callousness!

GUNN. But, honestly, I don't see anything wrong. He doesn't want it now, does he?

SHAWCROSS. If that's the line you take, I suppose there's no more to be said. . . . Get some stones!

[*While the others are burying the rucksack,* RANSOM *stoops and picks up* LAMP'S *snow-glasses, which he has left lying on the rocks at the back of the stage.*]

88

RANSOM. The first victim to my pride. If I had never asked him, he would not have come. The Abbot was perfectly right. My minor place in history is with the aberrant group of Caesars: the dullard murderers who hale the gentle from their beds of love and, with a quacking drum, escort them to the drowning ditch and the death in the desert. . . . [*To the others.*] You have forgotten these. [*Gives glasses.*] Hurry up. We must be getting on. Ian, will you change places with David?

> [*Music. They rope up in silence.* RANSOM *begins the traverse round the buttress, as the* CURTAIN *slowly falls.*]

[*Both* STAGE-BOXES *are illuminated. In the left-hand box,* STAGMANTLE *is at the microphone. In the right-hand box, the* A.'s *sit, listening.* MR A. *is playing Patience.* MRS A. *is darning socks.*]

STAGMANTLE. It is with the deepest regret that we have to announce the death of Mr Edward Lamp, a member of the F 6 Expedition. He was climbing along a ridge on the north face after a rare botanical specimen when he was caught by an avalanche and killed. He was twenty-four years of age.

In Edward Lamp, Science has lost one of her most brilliant recruits. At Cambridge he carried everything before him; and his career, so tragically cut short, promised to be of the highest distinction. He died as he had lived: in the service of his austere mistress. This is as he would have wished; and no man can do more. Nor could one design him a more fitting grave than among the alpine flowers he loved so passionately and with such understanding. . . .
[*Exit.*]

MRS A. [*moved*].
Death like his is right and splendid;
That is how life should be ended!
He cannot calculate nor dread

90

The mortifying in the bed,
Powers wasting day by day
While the courage ebbs away.
Ever-charming, he will miss
The insulting paralysis,
Ruined intellect's confusion,
Ulcer's patient persecution,
Sciatica's intolerance
And the cancer's sly advance;
Never hear, among the dead,
The rival's brilliant paper read,
Colleague's deprecating cough
And the praises falling off;
Never know how in the best
Passion loses interest;
Beauty sliding from the bone
Leaves the rigid skeleton.

MR A. If you had seen a dead man, you would not
Think it so beautiful to lie and rot;
I've watched men writhing on the dug-out floor
Cursing the land for which they went to war;
The joker cut off halfway through his story,
The coward blown involuntary to glory,
The steel butt smashing at the eyes that beg,
The stupid clutching at the shattered leg,
The twitching scarecrows on the rusty wire;
I've smelt Adonis stinking in the mire,
The puddle stolid round his golden curls,
Far from his precious mater and the girls;
I've heard the gas-case gargle, green as grass,

And, in the guns, Death's lasting animus.
Do you think it would comfort Lamp to know
The British Public mourns him so?
I tell you, he'd give his rarest flower
Merely to breathe for one more hour!
What is this expedition? He has died
To satisfy our smug suburban pride. . . .

[*The* STAGE-BOXES *are darkened.*]

ACT II

SCENE III

[*On F* 6. Camp A. *The left of stage is occupied by a tent, which is open at the end facing the audience. Behind it, to the right, the ground rises to a platform of rock, overhanging a precipice. It is early evening: during the dialogue which follows, the stage slowly darkens. Wind noises.*]
  [Ransom *and the* Doctor *are inside the tent, preparing a meal. The* Doctor *is cooking on the Primus stove.*]

Doctor. The wind's getting up again. It's going to be a bad night. . . . I wish those two would turn up.

Ransom. We can't expect them just yet. They're loaded, remember; and the going isn't easy.

Doctor. What was the psychrometer reading?

Ransom. 6·5.

Doctor. We're in for a lot more snow.

Ransom. It looks like it.

Doctor. And if it's bad down here, what's it going to be like up there on the arête?

Ransom [*smiling*]. Worse.

Doctor. M. F.—you can't start tomorrow!

Ransom. I must.

93

DOCTOR. If you try it in this weather, you haven't a chance!

RANSOM. We shall have a better chance tomorrow than the day after. Three days from now, there'd be none at all. We can't hang on here for more than four days: we haven't the stores.

DOCTOR. To try the arête in a blizzard is sheer madness!

RANSOM. Hasn't this whole climb been madness, Tom? We've done things in the last week which ought to have been planned and prepared for months. We've scrambled up here somehow, and now we must make a rush for it. . . . Whatever the weather is, I must leave for the summit tomorrow.

DOCTOR. Very well, M. F. You didn't bring me up here to argue with you. I won't. Just tell me what you want me to do.

RANSOM. Today is Tuesday. You'll wait for us here till Friday, at dawn. If we aren't back by then, you'll descend at once to Camp B, rest there as long as necessary and then carry out the evacuation of the mountain, as we arranged. . . . You understand, Tom? At once. There is to be no delay of any kind.

DOCTOR. You mean: no search party?

RANSOM. Nothing. If you like, I'll put that in writing. I forbid all useless risks. [*Smiling.*] I order you to return to England alive.

DOCTOR [*smiling*]. You'd better repeat that order to David personally.

RANSOM. David?

DOCTOR. He'll be second in command now, I suppose?
> [RANSOM *looks at him, smiles slightly and is silent.*]
Michael—you aren't thinking of taking him with you to the summit?

RANSOM. What if I am?

DOCTOR. Then you've chosen already?

RANSOM. Please don't question me now, Tom. Perhaps I have chosen. Perhaps I haven't, yet. We'll speak about it later. I can't tell you any more now.

DOCTOR. Very well, Michael. Just as you wish.
> [*A pause.*]

RANSOM. I know what you're thinking. Ian is steady, reliable, a first-class climber: David is only a brilliant amateur, a novice with an extraordinary flair, unsound, uneven, liable to moments of panic, without staying power. Yes, it's all true.

DOCTOR. Ian's wanted to do this climb with you more than he's ever wanted to do anything in his whole life.

RANSOM. I know. I've felt that, often. All these weeks, he's been on edge, straining every muscle and every nerve, never relaxing, torturing himself, denying himself, watching me like a dog waiting for a sign. . . . Already he's utterly exhausted; he's a feverish invalid. Take this sickness of his: as long as I've known him, Ian's never been sick on a mountain before. . . . You see, Tom, the ascent of F 6 represents, for Ian, a kind of triumph which he not only desires but of which he's desperately afraid. He

95

can't face it. He wants me to order him to face it. But if I do, it will destroy him.

DOCTOR [*after a pause*]. Perhaps you've right, M. F.... Yes, I think you are. But surely—you've admitted it yourself—David is afraid, too?

RANSOM. David is afraid of precipices, avalanches, cornices, falling stones. He is afraid of being killed; not of dying. He is not afraid of F 6, nor of himself.

DOCTOR. M. F.—The boys have their whole lives before them. Take me.

RANSOM [*after a pause*]. Yes, I'd thought of that, too. Thank you for asking me, Tom. I am very honoured.

DOCTOR. Oh, I know it's impossible, of course. I'm a fat old man. The crystal was right: I shall die in my bed.

RANSOM. You will die at the end of a long and useful life. You will have helped a great many people and comforted all whom you could not help.... But the Demon demands another kind of victim——

[*Whistling from* GUNN, *off. Enter* GUNN *and* SHAWCROSS, *R. Both of them are carrying stores. They cross the stage and enter the tent.*]

GUNN. Hullo, M. F.! Hullo, Doc.! Are we late for supper?

DOCTOR. No, it's just ready now.

[GUNN *and* SHAWCROSS *put down their loads.* SHAWCROSS *is much exhausted:* GUNN *fresh and lively.* RANSOM *lights the tent lantern.*]

GUNN. Gosh, I'm hungry! The altitude doesn't seem to affect *my* appetite. What is there to eat?

DOCTOR. Cocoa and oatmeal. [*Hands round rations.*]

96

GUNN. Oatmeal again!

DOCTOR. Perhaps you'd prefer a mutton chop?

GUNN. Don't, Tom, you swine! You make my mouth water! The first thing I'll do when I get back, I'll stand you dinner at Boulestin's. We'll start with two dozen Royal Whitstables——

DOCTOR. Oh, but David, Danish are much better!

GUNN. Just as you like. What about soup? Minestrone, I think?

DOCTOR. You have that. I prefer a really good tomato to anything.

GUNN. And now, what would you say to Lobster Newberg?

DOCTOR. I oughtn't to, really; but I can't resist.

GUNN. Good Lord! We've forgotten the wine!

SHAWCROSS [*bitterly*]. Must you always be talking about food?

GUNN. Was I? Sorry.

SHAWCROSS. Well, for God's sake, shut up then!

[*A pause.*]

DOCTOR. You're not eating anything, Ian.

SHAWCROSS. I don't want any, thanks.

DOCTOR. Take just a little. You must eat something, you know.

SHAWCROSS [*angrily*]. You heard me say No once. Are you going deaf?

RANSOM. Doctor's orders, Ian.

SHAWCROSS. All right, M. F. If you say so——

RANSOM [*handing him his mug of cocoa*]. Try this. It's good.

[SHAWCROSS *sips listlessly, putting the mug down almost at once.*]

GUNN. Thank God for my good dinner! Please may I get down? [*Pretending to strum on mandolin, sings:*]

Some have tennis-elbow
And some have housemaid's knee,
And some I know have got B.O.:
But these are not for me.
There's love the whole world over
Wherever you may be;
I had an aunt who loved a plant—
But you're my cup of tea!

DOCTOR [*laughing and applauding*]. Bravo!

[GUNN *bows.*]

You know, M. F., this reminds me of our first climb together, on the Meije. Do you remember that hut?

RANSOM. And our Primus that wouldn't light? Shall I ever forget it?

DOCTOR. And the fleas in the straw? Extraordinary the altitudes fleas can live at! Funny things, fleas. . . . If a flea were as big as a man, it could jump over St Paul's.

GUNN. When I was at school, I tried to keep a flea circus. But I could never train them to do anything at all. They're not really very intelligent.

DOCTOR. Perhaps you didn't go the right way about it. A man told me once that if——

SHAWCROSS [*passionately*]. Oh, for Christ's sake, shut up!

DOCTOR. Why, what's the matter, Ian?

SHAWCROSS. Do you expect me to sit listening to your drivel the whole night? Why do we keep pretending like this? Why don't we talk of what we're all thinking about? M. F., I've had about as much of this as I can stand! You've got to tell us now: which of us are you taking with you tomorrow?

DOCTOR. Steady, Ian! [*Puts a hand on his arm.*]

SHAWCROSS [*shaking him off*]. Let me alone, damn you! I wasn't talking to you! M. F., you've bloody well got to choose!

RANSOM. I have chosen, Ian. I'm taking David.

SHAWCROSS. Oh, my God! [*Pause.*] And I knew it all the time!

GUNN. Rotten luck, Ian. . . . I say, let me stay behind. . . . I don't mind, so very much. . . .

SHAWCROSS [*shouting*]. My God, do you think I'm going to crawl for favours to *you*, you little swine! You were always his favourite! I don't know how I've kept my hands off you so long! [*He tries to throttle* GUNN: *the* DOCTOR *seizes him.*]

DOCTOR. Ian, that's enough!

SHAWCROSS [*struggling free*]. Oh, I know—you're on his side, too! Do you think I haven't heard you whispering behind my back?

RANSOM. Is this what all your talk of loyalty amounts to, Ian? Tom and David have nothing to do with this. I am in charge of this expedition. If you have anything to complain of, be man enough to say so to me.

SHAWCROSS. I'm sorry, M. F. Forgive me. You're

99

quite right. I'm no damn good: I realize that now. You're all better men than I am. I had a pretty fine opinion of myself, once. I imagined I was indispensable. Even my admiration of you was only another kind of conceit. You were just an ideal of myself. But F 6 has broken me; it's shown me what I am—a rotten weakling. . . . I'll never give orders to anybody again.

RANSOM. No, Ian. You're wrong. F 6 hasn't broken you. It has made a man of you. You know yourself now. Go back to England with Tom. One day you will do something better worth while than this fool's errand on which David and I are going. I am giving you a harder job than mine.

SHAWCROSS [*hesitating*]. If I only could——! But you don't really believe it: I see you don't! No one will ever—— [*With rising excitement.*] They'd look at me and think—— No, I couldn't bear it! He failed—I can't—no, no—— I'll never let them! Never!

     [*He turns to rush out of the tent.*]

DOCTOR. Ian! [*They struggle at the tent flap; SHAWCROSS breaks free and runs across to the rock above the precipice; the others following.*]

RANSOM. Stop him!

GUNN. Ian, you fool, come back!

    [SHAWCROSS, *with a loud cry, springs over the precipice. The others reach the rock and stand peering down into the darkness. Gale noises and music.*]

CURTAIN

100

[*Both* STAGE-BOXES *are illuminated.*]
[*In the right-hand Box, the* A.*'s are listening.*
MRS A. *is adjusting the wireless:* MR A. *stands*
restlessly cleaning his pipe. In the left-hand Box,
the ANNOUNCER *is at the microphone.*]

ANNOUNCER. There is still no news of the British Ex-
    pedition to F 6. Fort George reports that a severe
    blizzard is general over the whole range. The grav-
    est anxiety is felt as to their safety——

MR A. Turn off the wireless; we are tired of descrip-
        tions of travel;
        We are bored by the exploits of amazing heroes;
        We do not wish to be heroes, nor are we likely
          to travel.
        We shall not penetrate the Arctic Circle
        And see the Northern Lights flashing far
          beyond Iceland;
        We shall not hear the prayer from the minaret
          echoing over Arabia
        Nor the surf on the coral atoll.

MRS A. Nor do we hope to be very distinguished;
        The embossed card of invitation is not for us;
        No photographers lurk at our door;
        The house-party and the grouse-moor we know
          by hearsay only;

We know of all these from the lending library
and the super cinema.

MR A. They excite us; but not very much. It is not our
life.

MRS A. For the skidding car and the neighbours' gossip
Are more terrifying to us than the snarling leap
of the tiger;
And the shop-fronts at Christmas a greater
marvel than Greece.

MR A. Let our fears and our achievements be sufficient
to our day.

MRS A. The luck at the bargain counter:

MR A. The giant marrow
grown on the allotment.

MRS A. Our moments of exaltation have not been extraordinary
But they have been real.

MR A. In the sea-side hotel, we experienced genuine
passion:

MRS A. Straying from the charabanc, under tremen-
dous beeches,
We were amazed at the profusion of bluebells
and the nameless birds;
And the Ghost Train and the switchback did
not always disappoint.

MR A. Turn off the wireless. Tune in to another station;
To the tricks of variety or the rhythm of jazz.
Let us roll back the carpet from the parlour floor
And dance to the wireless through the open
door.

102

[*They turn on the wireless and a dance band is
heard. The* A.*'s leave the box.*]

ANNOUNCER [*sings*].

Forget the Dead, what you've read,
All the errors and the terrors of the bed;
Dance, John, dance!
Ignore the Law, it's a bore,
Don't enumer all the rumours of a war;
Dance, John, dance!
Chin up!
Kiss me!
Atta Boy!
Dance till dawn among the ruins of a burning Troy!

Forget the Boss when he's cross,
All the bills and all the ills that make you toss:
Dance, John, dance!
Some get disease, others freeze,
Some have learned the way to turn themselves to
    trees;
Dance, John, etc.

[*The* STAGE-BOXES *are darkened.*]

ACT II

SCENE IV

[*On F* 6. *The Arête. Hurricane. Late afternoon.* RANSOM *supporting* GUNN.]

RANSOM. Steady. Lean on me.

GUNN. No, it's no use. I can't go any further. Help me down there, out of this bloody blizzard. [*They descend to a ledge.*] [*Collapsing.*] Thanks. But hurry. Go on, now, and reach the top. F 6 is a household word already. The nursemaids in the park go into raptures. The barber's chatter's full of nothing else. You mustn't disappoint them. In London now, they are unlocking the entrances to tubes. I should be still asleep but not alone. Toni was nice but very difficult. . . . Now no policeman will summons me again for careless driving. . . . They're flagging from the pits. . . . I cannot stop. . . . The brakes are gone. . . . Ian would be feeling as sick as a cat. . . . Where is that brake? Two hundred. . . . Christ, what banking! [*Dies.*]

RANSOM.

You always had good luck; it has not failed you
Even in this, your brightest escapade,

But extricates you now
From the most cruel cunning trap of all,
Sets you at large and leaves no trace behind,
Except this dummy.

O senseless hurricanes,
That waste yourselves upon the unvexed rock,
Find some employment proper to your powers,
Press on the neck of Man your murdering thumbs
And earn real gratitude! Astrologers,
Can you not scold the fated loitering star
To run to its collision and our end?
The Church and Chapel can agree in this,
The vagrant and the widow mumble for it
And those with millions belch their heavy prayers
To take away this luggage. Let the ape buy it
Or the insipid hen. Is Death so busy
That we must fidget in a draughty world
That's stale and tasteless; must we still kick our
    heels
And wait for his obsequious secretaries
To page Mankind at last and lead him
To the distinguished Presence?

CURTAIN

[The STAGE-BOXES *remain darkened. A voice from each is heard, in duet. They are like people speaking in their sleep.]*

LEFT BOX.   RIGHT BOX.

No news

                  Useless to wait

Too late

                  Their fate
                  We do not know

Snow on the pass

                  Alas

Nothing to report

                  Caught in the blizzard

Fought through the storm

                  Warm in our beds we
                     wonder

Thunder and hail

                  Will they fail? Will
                     they miss their
                     success?

Yes. They will die

                  We sigh. We cannot
                     aid

They fade from our mind

                  They find no breath

But Death

ACT II

SCENE V

[*F 6. The stage rises steeply, in a series of rock terraces, to the small platform at the back which forms the summit of the mountain. Blizzard. Gathering darkness.*]

> [*In the front of the stage* RANSOM *is struggling upwards. After a few numbed movements, he falls exhausted. Music throughout. The light now fades into complete darkness. The voices of the* CHORUS, *dressed in the habit of the monks from the glacier monastery, are heard.*]

CHORUS.

Let the eye of the traveller consider this country
  and weep,
For toads croak in the cisterns; the aqueducts choke
  with leaves:
The highways are out of repair and infested with
  thieves:
The ragged population are crazy for lack of sleep:
Our chimneys are smokeless; the implements rust
  in the field
And our tall constructions are felled.

Over our empty playgrounds the wet winds sough;
The crab and the sandhopper possess our aban-
  doned beaches;

Upon our gardens the dock and the darnel encroaches;
The crumbling lighthouse is circled with moss like a muff;
The weasel inhabits the courts and the sacred places;
Despair is in our faces.

[*The summit of the mountain is illuminated, revealing a veiled, seated figure.*]

For the Dragon has wasted the forest and set fire to the farm;
He has mutilated our sons in his terrible rages
And our daughters he has stolen to be victims of his dissolute orgies;
He has cracked the skulls of our children in the crook of his arm;
With the blast of his nostrils he scatters death through the land;
We are babes in his hairy hand.

O, when shall the deliverer come to destroy this dragon?
For it is stated in the prophecies that such a one shall appear,
Shall ride on a white horse and pierce his heart with a spear;
Our elders shall welcome him home with trumpet and organ,
Load him with treasure, yes, and our most beautiful maidenhead

He shall have for his bed.

[*The veiled* FIGURE *on the summit raises its hand. There is a fanfare of trumpets. The* DRAGON, *in the form of* JAMES RANSOM, *appears. He wears full ceremonial dress, with orders. He is illuminated by a spot-light. The* CHORUS, *throughout the whole scene, remain in semi-darkness.*]

[*As* JAMES *appears, the* CHORUS *utter a cry of dismay.* JAMES *bows to the* FIGURE.]

JAMES. I am sorry to say that our civilizing mission has been subject to grave misinterpretations. Our critics have been unhelpful and, I am constrained to add, unfair. The powers which I represent stand unequivocally for peace. We have declared our willingness to conclude pacts of non-aggression with all of you—on condition, of course, that our demands are reasonably met. During the past few years we have carried unilateral disarmament to the utmost limits of safety; others, whom I need not specify, have unfortunately failed to follow our example. We now find ourselves in a position of inferiority which is intolerable to the honour and interests of a great power; and in self-defence we are reluctantly obliged to take the necessary measures to rectify the situation. We have constantly reiterated our earnest desire for peace; but in the face of unprovoked aggression I must utter a solemn warning to you all that we are prepared to defend ourselves to the fullest extent of our forces against all comers.

111

[JAMES *is seated. Duet from the* darkened
STAGE-BOXES.]

DUET.   Him who comes to set us free
Save whoever it may be,
From the fountain's thirsty snare,
From the music in the air,
From the tempting fit of slumber,
From the odd unlucky number,
From the riddle's easy trap,
From the ignorance of the map,
From the locked forbidden room,
From the Guardian of the Tomb,
From the siren's wrecking call,
Save him now and save us all.

[*Flourish on the wood-wind.* MICHAEL RANSOM
steps into the light which surrounds the Dragon
JAMES. *He still wears his climbing things but is
without helmet, goggles or ice-axe.*]

JAMES. Michael! Why have you come here? What do
you want?

RANSOM. Hardly very friendly, are you?

JAMES. What is it this time? We are grown men
now.

RANSOM. There is no time to lose. I have come to make
you a most important proposition.

JAMES. Which I accept—on my own conditions.

[*At his signal a complete set of life-size chessmen
appear. The chief pieces on* JAMES' *side are*
STAGMANTLE, ISABEL *and the* GENERAL; *and
on* MICHAEL's, SHAWCROSS, GUNN *and*

LAMP. *All have masks which partially disguise them.*]

Before we continue, if any of you have any questions you would like to put either to my colleagues or myself, we shall be delighted to do our best to answer them.

[*As each character answers his question, he or she removes the mask.*]

MR A. [*from stage-box*]. Why is my work so dull?

GENERAL. That is a most insubordinate remark. Every man has his job in life, and all he has to think about is doing it as well as it can be done. What is needed is loyalty, not criticism. Think of those climbers up on F 6. No decent food. No fires. No nice warm beds. Do you think *they* grumble? You ought to be ashamed of yourself.

MRS A. Why doesn't my husband love me any more?

ISABEL. My dear, I'm terribly sorry for you. I do understand. But aren't you being just a teeny-weeny bit morbid? Now think of those young climbers up there on F 6. They're not worrying about their love affairs. [*Archly.*] And I'm sure they must have several. Of course, I know people like you and me can't do big things like that, but we can find little simple everyday things which help to take us out of ourselves. Try to learn Bridge or get a book from the lending library. Reorganize your life. I know it won't be easy at first, but I'm sure if you stick to it you'll find you won't brood so much. And you'll be ever so much happier.

MR A. Why have I so little money?

STAGMANTLE. Ah, I was expecting that one! I'm a practical man like yourself, and as it happens I'm a rich one, so I ought to know something about money. I know there are far too many people who have too little. It's a damned shame, but there it is. That's the world we live in. But speaking quite seriously as a business man, I can tell you that money doesn't necessarily bring happiness. In fact, the more you worry about it, the unhappier you are. The finest and happiest man I ever met— he's leading the expedition up F 6 at the moment— doesn't care a brass button for money, and never has. So my advice is: Get all the cash you can and stick to it, but don't worry.

MR A. and⎫
MRS A.   ⎬ Why were we born?

JAMES. That's a very interesting question, and I'm not sure I can answer it myself. But I know what my brother, the climber, thinks. When we take, he said to me once, the life of the individual, with its tiny circumscribed area in space and time, and measure it against the geological epochs, the gigantic movements of history and the immensity of the universe, we are forced, I think, to the conclusion that, taking the large view, the life of the individual has no real existence or importance apart from the great whole; that he is here indeed but to serve for his brief moment his community, his race, his planet, his universe; and then, passing on the torch

114

of life undiminished to others, his little task accomplished, to die and be forgotten.

RANSOM. You're not being fair to me.

JAMES. Keep to your world. I will keep to mine.

[*The chess game begins. Complete silence, accompanied only by a drum roll. At intervals* JAMES *or* MICHAEL *says:'Check!'*]

JAMES. Check!

RANSOM [*looking for the first time towards the summit and seeing the figure*]. Look!

JAMES. Mate! I've won!

[*The* FIGURE *shakes its head.*]

RANSOM [*his eyes still fixed upon it*]. But was the victory real?

JAMES [*half rises to his feet, totters: in a choking voice*]. It was not Virtue—it was not Knowledge—it was Power! [*Collapses.*]

CHORUS. What have you done? What have you done?

You have killed, you have murdered her favourite son!

[*Confusion. During the following speeches,* STAGMANTLE, *the* GENERAL *and* ISABEL *jostle each other, jump on each other's shoulders to get a better hearing and behave in general like the Marx brothers.*]

STAGMANTLE. The whole of England is plunged into mourning for one of her greatest sons; but it is a sorrow tempered with pride, that once again

115

Englishmen have been weighed in the balance and not found wanting.

ISABEL. At this hour, the thoughts of the whole nation go out to a very brave and very lonely woman in a little South country cottage; already a widow and now a bereaved mother.

GENERAL. I am no climber; but I know courage when I see it. He was a brave man and courage is the greatest quality a man can have.

STAGMANTLE. Sport transcends all national barriers, and it is some comfort to realize that this tragedy has brought two great nations closer together.

ISABEL. In the face of this terrible tragedy, one is almost tempted to believe in the grim old legend of the Demon.

[*A figure having the shape of the* ABBOT, *wearing a monk's habit and a judge's wig and holding the crystal in his hands, is illuminated at a somewhat higher level of the stage.*]

ABBOT. I am truly sorry for this young man, but I must ask for the Court to be cleared.

[*Exeunt* SHAWCROSS, LAMP *and* GUNN.]

[*A Blues.* MONKS *enter with a stretcher,* JAMES' *body is carried in slow procession round the stage and away into the darkness.*]

STAGMANTLE and ISABEL.

Stop all the clocks, cut off the telephone,
Prevent the dog from barking with a juicy bone,
Silence the pianos and with muffled drum
Bring out the coffin, let the mourners come.

Let aeroplanes circle moaning overhead
Scribbling on the sky the message: He is dead.
Put crepe bows round the white necks of the public
    doves.
Let the traffic policemen wear black cotton gloves.

Hold up your umbrellas to keep off the rain
From Doctor Williams while he opens a vein;
Life, he pronounces, it is finally extinct.
Sergeant, arrest that man who said he winked!

Shawcross will say a few words sad and kind
To the weeping crowds about the Master-Mind,
While Lamp with a powerful microscope
Searches their faces for a sign of hope.

And Gunn, of course, will drive the motor-hearse:
None could drive it better, most would drive it worse.
He'll open up the throttle to its fullest power
And drive him to the grave at ninety miles an hour.

ABBOT. Please be seated, Mr Ransom. I hope everything has been arranged here to your satisfaction?

RANSOM. I didn't do it! I swear I didn't touch him! It
wasn't my fault! [*Pointing to* FIGURE.] The Demon
gave the sign! The Demon is real!

ABBOT. In that case, we will call the victims of his
pride. Call Ian Shawcross!

CHORUS. Ian Shawcross!

    [SHAWCROSS *appears. He is bloodstained and pale.*]

RANSOM. I've had about as much of this as I can stand.
You've got to tell them! I hate to bother you with
this sort of thing.

117

SHAWCROSS. I'm afraid you haven't succeeded very well.

RANSOM. You mean, you *did* see something? If you hadn't, you mightn't believe me.

SHAWCROSS. Oh, for Christ's sake, shut up! If what you've done amuses you, I'm glad. I'm not very tolerant, I'm afraid.   [*Exit.*]

ABBOT. Call David Gunn!

CHORUS. David Gunn!

> [*Enter* DAVID GUNN, *pale and covered with snow. His face is entirely without features.*]

RANSOM. David, you saw what happened?

GUNN. Didn't I just? You did it beautifully. It was first class!

RANSOM. You sound pleased!

GUNN. Of course I'm pleased! Who wouldn't be!

RANSOM. David, there's something I *must* tell you——

> [*Exit* GUNN.]

ABBOT. Call Edward Lamp!

CHORUS. Edward Lamp! Edward Lamp! Edward Lamp!

LAMP'S VOICE [*far away, off*]. I'm all right.

RANSOM [*shouts*]. Teddy, what did *you* see?

LAMP'S VOICE. If I told you, you wouldn't be any the wiser.

RANSOM. You're on their side, too! Is this all your talk of loyalty amounts to?

MRS A. O, what's the use of your pretending
As if Life had a chance of mending?
There will be nothing to remember
But the fortnight in August or early September.

118

Mr A. Home to supper and to bed.

It'll be like this till we are dead.

[DOCTOR *appears.*]

RANSOM. Tom!

DOCTOR. Just tell me what you want me to do.

RANSOM. I can't face it!

DOCTOR. Perhaps you are right. The Demon demands another kind of victim. Ask the crystal.

[*Exit* DOCTOR.]

ABBOT. You wish to appeal to the crystal, Mr Ransom? Do not ask at once, but think it over.

RANSOM. We haven't a moment to lose. I appeal to the crystal.

ABBOT. Very well, since you wish it, I obey you. [*Looks into crystal.*]

[*Music. Duet from stage-boxes, the* A.'s *sing.*]

MRS A. and MR A.

Make us kind,

Make us of one mind,

Make us brave,

Save, save, save, save.

ABBOT. Mr Ransom, I did you an injustice. I thought I understood your temptation, but I was wrong. The temptation is not the Demon. If there were no Demon, there would be no temptation.

RANSOM. What have I said? I didn't mean it! Forgive me! It was all my fault. F 6 has shown me what I am. I'm a coward and a prig. I withdraw the charge.

ABBOT. Such altruism, Mr Ransom, is uncommon in

one of your race. But I am afraid it is too late now. The case is being brought by the Crown. [*Turning to the* FIGURE *on the summit.*] Have you anything to say in your defence? [*Pause.*] You realize the consequences of silence? [*Pause.*] As long as the world endures there must be law and order. [*To* CHORUS.] Gentlemen, consider your verdict.

CHORUS.

At last the secret is out, as it always must come in
    the end,
The delicious story is ripe to tell to the intimate friend;
Over the tea-cups and in the square the tongue has
    its desire;
Still waters run deep, my dear, there's never smoke
    without fire.

Behind the corpse in the reservoir, behind the ghost
    on the links,
Behind the lady who dances and the man who mad-
    ly drinks,
Under the look of fatigue, the attack of migraine
    and the sigh
There is always another story, there is more than
    meets the eye.

For the clear voice suddenly singing, high up in the
    convent wall,
The scent of the elder bushes, the sporting prints in
    the hall,
The croquet matches in summer, the handshake, the
    cough, the kiss,

There is always a wicked secret, a private reason
for this.

ABBOT. Have you considered your verdict?

RANSOM. Stop!

[*He rushes up to the summit and places himself
in front of the* FIGURE, *with his arms out-
stretched, as if to protect it.*]

RANSOM. No one shall ever——! I couldn't bear it! I'll
never let them! Never!

ABBOT [*to* CHORUS]. Guilty or not guilty?

CHORUS [*all pointing to the* FIGURE]. Guilty!

GENERAL. Die for England!

ISABEL. Honour!

STAGMANTLE. Service!

GENERAL. Duty!

ISABEL. Sacrifice!

ALL. Die for England.

VOICE. Ostnia.

ALL. England. England. England.

MRS A. and MR A. Die for us!

[*Thunder and the roar of an avalanche are heard.
All lights are extinguished below; only the*
FIGURE *and* RANSOM *remain illuminated.*
RANSOM *turns to the* FIGURE, *whose draperies
fall away, revealing* MRS RANSOM *as a young
mother.*]

RANSOM. Mother!

MOTHER [MRS RANSOM]. My boy! At last!

[*He falls at her feet with his head in her lap. She
strokes his hair.*]

121

CHORUS. Acts of injustice done
      Between the setting and the rising sun
      In history lie like bones, each one.
MRS RANSOM. Still the dark forest, quiet the deep,
      Softly the clock ticks, baby must sleep!
      The Pole star is shining, bright the Great Bear,
      Orion is watching, high up in the air.
CHORUS. Memory sees them down there,
      Paces alive beside his fear
      That's slow to die and still here.
MRS RANSOM. Reindeer are coming to drive you
            away
      Over the snow on an ebony sleigh,
      Over the mountain and over the sea
      You shall go happy and handsome and free.
CHORUS. The future, hard to mark,
      Of a world turning in the dark
      Where ghosts are walking and dogs bark.
MRS RANSOM. Over the green grass pastures there
      You shall go hunting the beautiful deer,
      You shall pick flowers, the white and the blue,
      Shepherds shall flute their sweetest for you.
CHORUS. True, Love finally is great,
      Greater than all; but large the hate,
      Far larger than Man can ever estimate.
MRS RANSOM. And in the castle tower above,
      The princess' cheek burns red for your love,
      You shall be king and queen of the land,
      Happy for ever, hand in hand.
CHORUS. But between the day and night

The choice is free to all, and light
Falls equally on black and white.

[*During the first verse of the Chorale which follows, the light fades from the summit, so that the
stage is completely darkened. Then, after a moment, the entire stage is gradually illuminated by
the rising sun. The stage is empty, except for the
body of* RANSOM, *who lies dead on the summit of
the mountain.*]

HIDDEN CHORUS. Free now from indignation,
Immune from all frustration
He lies in death alone;
Now he with secret terror
And every minor error
Has also made Man's weakness known.

Whom history has deserted,
These have their power exerted,
In one convulsive throe;
With sudden drowning suction
Drew him to his destruction.
[*Cresc.*] But they to dissolution go.

SLOW CURTAIN

2/14/40
1/2/46.
7/3/51.

123